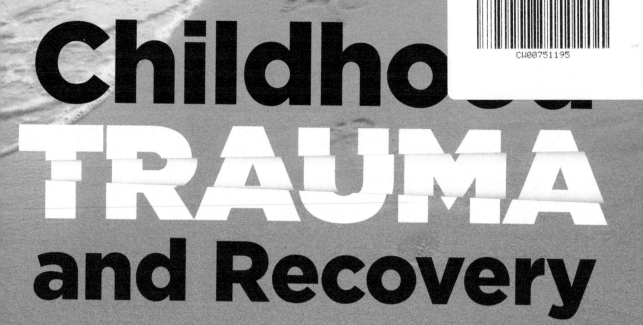

Childhood TRAUMA and Recovery

A Child-Centred Approach to Healing Early Years Abuse

**Mary Walsh
and Neil Thompson**

Child Trauma and Recovery
A child-centred approach to healing early years abuse

Published by:
Pavilion Publishing and Media Ltd
Blue Sky Offices
Cecil Pashley Way
Shoreham by Sea
West Sussex
BN43 5FF
Tel: 01273 434 943
Email: info@pavpub.com

Published 2019

A catalogue record for this book is available from the British Library.

ISBN: 978-1-912755-55-4

Pavilion is the leading training and development provider and publisher in the health, social care and allied fields, providing a range of innovative training solutions underpinned by sound research and professional values. We aim to put our customers first, through excellent customer service and value.

Authors: Mary Walsh and Neil Thompson
Production editor: Mike Benge, Pavilion Publishing and Media Ltd
Cover design: Phil Morash, Pavilion Publishing and Media Ltd
Page layout and typesetting: Phil Morash, Pavilion Publishing and Media Ltd
Printing: Severn

Contents

About the authors... 3

Preface 4

Acknowledgements 7

Introduction 9

Chapter 1: The roots of the approach 13

Chapter 2: Developing the approach 39

Chapter 3: The journey of ideas 61

Chapter 4: The terror of abuse 83

Chapter 5: The importance of recovery 97

Chapter 6: Being child centred 117

Chapter 7: Equality, diversity and inclusion 133

Chapter 8: Caring for the carers 151

Conclusion.. 167

References... 173

Appendix I: Guide to Further Learning......................... 183

Appendix II: The Children's Stories.............................. 189

Appendix III: The Mary Walsh Approach in a Nutshell........................... 197

About the authors

Mary Walsh was a child protection social worker in the early 1980s, during which time she gained valuable experience and expertise in communicating with children who had been sexually abused. She pioneered techniques to help them to demonstrate what had happened to them. In 1987 she co-founded SACCS and ran it for 25 years. It was originally set up to help children express their distress and recover from their trauma. Later, to meet the needs of some very vulnerable children who could no longer live at home, she started SACCS Care, a residential therapeutic project focused on children's recovery.

She has trained professionals including police, psychiatrists, psychologists and social workers, among others, and has delivered keynote presentations at international conferences.

Now retired, she is a founder member and trustee of the Institute of Recovery from Childhood Trauma.

Dr Neil Thompson is an independent writer, educator and adviser, with expertise in social work and the wider field of human relations and well-being. He has held full or honorary professorships at four UK universities. He has over 40 years' experience in the helping professions as a practitioner, manager, educator and consultant.

He has 44 books to his name, including several bestsellers. He has also been involved in developing a range of e-books and other learning resources, including training manuals, DVDs and e-learning courses (www.avenuemediasolutions. com). He also tutors an online professional development programme based on principles of self-directed learning (www.apdp.org.uk).

He has qualifications in social work, management (MBA), training and development, mediation and dispute resolution, as well as a first-class honours degree in Social Sciences, a doctorate (PhD) and a higher doctorate (DLitt). Neil is a Fellow of the Chartered Institute of Personnel and Development and the Royal Society of Arts. He was previously the editor of the US-based international journal *Illness, Crisis & Loss*. He currently edits the free e-zine, **THE** *humansolutions* **BULLETIN** (www.humansolutions.org.uk/bulletin). His website and blog are at www.NeilThompson.info.

Preface

For many years it was assumed that children who had been sexually abused would 'get over it' if they were removed from the perpetrator's grasp and placed with loving and supportive carers. The pioneering work of Mary Walsh and her colleagues has helped us to realise that the reality is far more complex. We are now much more aware of the significance of trauma and the dangers of not recognising its impact on children and young people who have been abused. Thanks to the work of Mary's team we now know that, if trauma issues are not addressed, the net result can be that the children in effect traumatise others (for example, through highly sexualised behaviour), often leading to placement breakdown after placement breakdown. This then creates a vicious circle in which the child is further traumatised. The insights of Mary Walsh and her team have played a major role in not only raising awareness of such dangers, but also in developing sophisticated ways of helping the children concerned to recover from their harmful experiences as far as possible and a sound basis of learning for a wide range of child care professionals.

The authors of this book have known each other for over 25 years and share a commitment to doing what is best for abused children, particularly in relation to helping them overcome the ill effects of trauma. We are honoured to have been able to make a contribution to understanding childhood trauma and promoting recovery from it. This book is based on the two authors reviewing together the work that has been done under Mary's leadership to promote better-informed approaches to tackling the adverse effects of abuse-related trauma. What we have tried to do is to develop a clear and helpful picture of the philosophy on which Mary's work has been based, the impact it has had on theory and practice in this area and the lessons that can be learned.

This is in no sense a definitive work. We still have a long way to go before we can claim to have a comprehensive theory of childhood trauma as a response to abuse (particularly sexual abuse). However, we have made significant strides forward in developing our understanding as a platform for informing our practice, and that is what this book is intended to reflect. It serves two basic functions. On the one hand it provides a very helpful text on childhood trauma and recovery that will be an invaluable guide to this important theory base for an extensive range of child care professionals and students in training. On the other hand, it should also serve as a helpful guide to practice, offering insights that not only inform theoretical understanding but also provide a platform for developing practical approaches to the challenges involved.

There is an immense and growing literature on childhood trauma, particularly in relation to what have come to be referred to as ACEs (adverse childhood experiences). Given the scope and fast-growing nature of this field, this book cannot be seen as in any way comprehensive or exhaustive. Rather, what we are offering here is an overview of the significance of abuse-related childhood trauma, with particular emphasis on the work done by Mary Walsh and her colleagues over almost 30 years. The Mary Walsh Approach, as we shall be calling it here, has made a distinctive contribution to our understanding and has directly influenced the practice of a large number of childcare practitioners nationally and internationally.

This approach emerged from Mary's key role in developing SACCS (Sexual Abuse Childcare Consultancy Services), an organisation that, for over a quarter of a century, provided consultancy, training, expert witness services, family-style residential care and fostering services to a wide range of children who had been traumatised by sexual abuse. The SACCS team was also responsible for publishing a range of important books on different aspects of this demanding area of childcare practice (see the *Guide to further learning* on page 183 for details).

It is based on a three-dimensional framework that incorporates:

- **Individual therapy**. While there will be common themes across the experience of childhood trauma, each child will have their own story; their own unique and distinctive experience and what it means to them. To make progress in recovery, it is essential that the specific needs and circumstances of each child are understood and taken into consideration. Individual therapy therefore has a key role to play.

- **Life story work**. Revisiting and making sense of the child's journey in life so far can help to provide a platform of understanding for the child, a meaningful self-narrative that helps to move from the status of 'victim' to 'survivor', with all the personal growth and empowerment that this entails. Identity is, of course, a key aspect of any person's life (Thompson, 2017a), but this is especially true for children and young people who are still trying to find their way in the world, still trying to forge a sense of self that they are happy with. Adverse childhood experiences are likely to present significant obstacles to the development of a positive identity. Skilled life story work has an important role to play in helping to counter such adverse experiences and put in place a foundation for more helpful identity formation (Rose & Philpot, 2005; Rose, 2017).

- **Therapeutic parenting**. Foster care is intended to provide, as a minimum, the three Ss of safety, shelter and sustenance. However, appropriately trained and supported foster carers can provide much more than this by offering not only a safe haven, but also an environment in which the child can grow, can be supported through the adverse consequences of trauma (including acting out and/or sexualised behaviour) and be 'held' emotionally (Weld, 2009), so that the insecurity they have experienced to date can gradually be replaced by a firmer basis of security – physical and emotional. This is very challenging work that requires skilled and experienced foster carers who have a sound understanding of the issues involved.

A key aspect of the Mary Walsh Approach is the need to understand these three elements as parts of a dynamic set of interactions, rather than static components to be considered separately from one another. For example, what emerges from life story work could impinge on individual therapy and possibly have an effect on the fostering support needed.

As we proceed through the book, each of the chapters will cast fuller light on these issues and provide a fuller basis of understanding. We very much hope that you will be able to use this understanding to make you as well equipped as possible to play an important role in helping children along their journey of recovery.

This book should be valuable to anyone working with traumatised children, including social workers, nurses, therapists, foster carers, residential care workers, play workers, teachers and classroom assistants, plus people training to fulfil any of these roles. We hope and trust that you will find what the book has to offer beneficial and worthwhile.

Acknowledgements

We are grateful to the team at Pavilion Publishing for giving us the opportunity to bring awareness of the Mary Walsh Approach to a wider audience and thereby play a part in tackling the major challenges presented by child sexual abuse and trauma.

Mary would like to thank first and foremost all the children she has worked with who have taught her, sometimes painstakingly, all that she knows today. Every child's experience is unique but, taken together, they have built into a compelling picture of how to meet their needs and help them to recover. Mary never ceases to be amazed at their courage, their resilience in the face of overwhelming events and their willingness to make the journey to recovery. It has been a joy and a privilege to work with these children and she thanks them from the bottom of her heart.

Second, Mary extends a big thank you to all the staff who have worked with her over the years, for their dedication, commitment and passion, often in very difficult circumstances, and for their part in helping her to achieve her vision.

Mary also wants to thank Neil Thompson, without whom this book would not have been possible, for his persistence and constant belief in her.

Lastly, and most importantly, Mary thanks her family; her rock, whose unwavering support has sustained her over the years.

Neil would like to thank his wife, Dr Sue Thompson, for the various ways in which she supports him in his work and in his life more broadly, and his daughter, Anna, for her unstinting practical and technical support.

Neil would also like to thank the wide range of excellent child care practitioners he has had the good fortune to work with over the years and learn so much from (while also learning a lot from those who were far from excellent!).

Neil is grateful to Dr Viv Dacre of Wrexham Glyndŵr University for unstinting colleagueship in joint efforts to promote positive child care practice.

In addition, Neil wants to express his gratitude to the members of his online learning community, the Avenue Professional Development Programme, for the stimulating and rewarding discussion that they consistently generate.

Introduction

Until the 1960s child abuse received little or no attention; the idea that so many people could harm children (and especially parents harming their own children) was something that the public (and professionals) found very difficult to accept. It took a long time before the reality and extent of abuse came to be accepted as fact (Corby *et al*, 2013). The 1980s saw an intensification of interest in abuse as a result of scandals relating to the sexual abuse of children. The 'Cleveland affair', in which large numbers of children in the north east of England were deemed to have been sexually abused, garnered considerable media interest (Bell, 1988; Campbell, 1988). We later saw a growing awareness of institutional abuse – children and young people being abused in children's homes, residential schools and even foster care (Waterhouse, 2000). Gradually, the idea that the abuse of children was a very occasional occurrence, and mainly carried out by strangers, came to be replaced by the recognition that child abuse is a major social problem (Thompson, 2017b).

So, despite the relative neglect of child abuse as a social problem in the past, for some time now we have had a high level of awareness of abuse and the need for sophisticated systems of child protection. Nonetheless, it is quite clear that we still have a long way to go before we can claim to have reached a satisfactory position. While immense resources are invested in safeguarding children from harm and dealing with the aftermath of abuse, it would be foolhardy to say that we are doing enough to prevent children from being abused and supporting them through the traumatic consequences. This book will help to establish why it is important that we do much more by showing just how much harm abuse and trauma can do. It is to be hoped that it will provide an important basis of understanding from which to develop high-quality professional practice.

This book is divided into eight chapters. The first, entitled 'Developing the model', reflects a historical development theme. It charts the development of the Mary Walsh Approach and shows how the development of her work has reflected the wider development of social policy responses to child abuse. The second chapter, 'Making a difference in practice', focuses on how the organisation Mary co-founded flourished for over 25 years despite various obstacles and setbacks, and sets out the main elements of the approach that Mary and her colleagues developed, which has been the mainstay of the work undertaken. The third chapter describes the journey of ideas. This involves drawing out the key concepts and frameworks that have informed the development of the underlying philosophy and the Mary Walsh Approach which flows from it.

Chapter 4 explores the horror of abuse and makes it clear how harmful abuse is, not least in terms of its traumatic consequences. This chapter also shows how significant trauma is in relation to a wide range of social problems, not least adult mental health. Chapter 5 places great emphasis on the importance of recovery and establishes the need for a structured approach to helping children 'get over' the abuse. This chapter challenges the oversimplified notion that placing abused children in safe and loving places will be enough to allow them to put their abusive experiences behind them and move on positively with their lives. In this regard the chapter runs counter to much of the traditional child care 'wisdom', which has tended to neglect the need for a structured and systematic approach to trauma recovery.

Being child centred is a value that has underpinned the Mary Walsh Approach right from the start, and has also been a cornerstone of the work of so many people who have adopted this approach. Chapter 6 therefore explores what is involved in taking this notion seriously in our work with children and young people.

Chapter 7 is concerned with equality, diversity and inclusion, recognising the need for professional practice across the board to be sensitive to issues of discrimination and oppression, with recovery from trauma being no exception. Chapter 8 is entitled 'Getting the people issues right'. This final chapter examines the importance of getting staffing issues right. If staff are not adequately trained, supported and valued, then they cannot be expected to give of their best in working with abused and traumatised children. Indeed, if such matters are not given the attention they deserve, the result can be stress and distress for children and adults alike, potentially undermining all the good work that has been done.

Interspersed among the chapters are some short 'practice focus' examples that highlight actual case scenarios Mary has been involved in. These cameos (with the names changed to protect confidentiality, of course) are provided to help bring to life some of the important points we are making in the text.

The book also contains three appendices. The first is a guide to further learning to support the development of ongoing learning about these sensitive matters. It contains information about relevant books, journals and websites. The inclusion of this guide helps to emphasise how complex a field of study and professional practice this is, and therefore how important it is to continue learning and not become complacent about our knowledge base. The second is a set of 'stories', brief cameos that highlight the experiences of many of the children that the approach described in this book has helped. These are authentic, brief accounts of real-life cases involving abused children. Each story is accompanied by questions that can be used by individual readers to encourage further thought and learning and/or by tutors and trainers who may want to use the materials as the basis of classroom discussions.

The third appendix is a brief summary of the Mary Walsh Approach, an overview of the key points that underpin what has proven to be a very effective and influential approach.

We live in an age in which immense and sustained efforts are made to prevent child abuse, to detect and investigate it and to remove children from harm. These are all essential elements of a commitment to safeguarding children from harm and therefore very worthwhile endeavours. However, what has received far less attention is the aftermath of abuse. We have begun to develop a much fuller understanding of how abuse, particularly sexual abuse, results in trauma and how that trauma can devastate the lives of not only the children and young people concerned, but also the people who care for them. This book provides a clear and helpful account of the main elements of the knowledge base we have developed, how it can be used in practice and what areas of further development we need to pursue. As such, it should make an important contribution to education and training in this demanding field and provide a basis for developing the most effective practice we can in such difficult circumstances.

Chapter 1: The roots of the approach

This chapter tells the story of how the Mary Walsh Approach, with its three-dimensional model, was developed. It charts how personal, professional and political factors combined to shape the emergence of a sophisticated and coherent approach to addressing the major consequences of trauma for children who have been abused.

Mary's own journey began in her childhood and led to the development of her pioneering work in the child care field. It is, of course, a personal journey, but it reflects the wider social history of UK responses to the problems of child abuse. It offers a useful historical backdrop that can cast considerable light on current policies, practices and outlooks. We begin by looking at how Mary's own experiences of childhood pain helped to sensitise her to the suffering experienced by abused children. This then leads us into a discussion of a range of other important factors in the development of her approach.

Sensitivity to children's pain

There are, of course, many examples on record of people who have emerged from negative childhood experiences to achieve great things, driven forward by their own motivation to draw out positives and make a real difference as a result of their adverse experiences. Mary's own experience reflects this pattern, with the roots of her pioneering work being in her own unhappy childhood. At the age of seven she was sent away to boarding school. Although she felt her parents thought they were doing the best thing for her, she herself perceived it as a rejection by her family. The result was abject misery as a result of the peer and adult bullying which was an ongoing experience until she reached the age of 15, making Mary what she described as a 'hurt' child. It was these events that informed her of the terrible effects of rejection, abandonment, torment and the lack of safety and security for children. As well as being able to empathise and sympathise with hurt children, Mary has also been able to walk the same path and use her own experiences as a blueprint to understand and work alongside children and their carers. It is important to recognise at this point that Mary's early life experiences were not consumed by abuse and mistreatment. Her internalised hurt was real for her, in the sense of the school placement; its journey and the separation from her family. Mary firmly believes that if the school placement had not been made, then these all too difficult experiences would not have affected her life in the same way. Consequently, her life-long vocation with the recovery of traumatised children may not have featured. Mary's childhood experiences were not abusive as such, however they were sufficiently difficult and painful for her to develop a strong commitment to helping children deal with their hurt, suffering and confusion. This has been at the heart of her determination to protect and support traumatised children.

Key point

The old adage that 'the child is father to the man', despite its gender bias, is a significant insight. Mary's personal experiences of being a hurt child shaped her whole career and, with it, her sense of identity. Each of us, whether abused or not, will have much of our adult sensibility shaped by our childhood experiences. This understanding is at the heart of trauma recovery efforts.

Mary began her career in social work as a welfare assistant working with older and disabled people and families with complex needs. This eventually led to a role that involved working with a full caseload. Many of these cases were complex childcare issues. She found that her own childhood experiences had given her a special sensitivity to children's pain and indeed to the pain of the adults involved – clearly an important consideration for working with abused children.

After qualifying as a social worker, it became apparent that many girls between the ages of 11 and 14 were coming to her attention, and that these children had been sexually abused. While the idea that sexual abuse would be affecting a certain proportion of teenaged and pre-teen girls is now widely accepted within the professional practice arena, it has to be remembered that, at the time, this was a new and highly unsettling realisation – it was a development that challenged much about the assumptions we made about the risks to children, a challenge that was to have major consequences over the coming decades.

Mary started running an experiential group for these young girls and the success of this work heralded a series of future groups across the county over the next few years. This was an innovative introduction of direct work with children who had been severely hurt by the actions of those closest to them. This was at a time when the significance of sexual abuse was emerging as a new dimension of child abuse, of what had previously been understood to be predominantly a matter of 'non-accidental injury', with its emphasis on physical harm (Corby *et al*, 2013).

After a year as a qualified social worker Mary started work in the UK's first child protection team, which was called the Special Unit. As the only woman in what had previously been an all-male team, Mary found herself responding to and investigating a high number of sexual abuse investigations. In the early 1980s, following the emergence of the women's movement, the culture in the country was such that, in the area of sexual abuse, men were felt to be too dangerous to be allowed to work with vulnerable children (see the discussion of sexism in Chapter 7).

This combination of circumstances (sexual abuse emerging as a major problem and being the only woman in the only specialist unit in the country) made Mary a de facto leading practice expert in the field of sexual abuse, one of the very few people to have developed the expertise at that point in time. From this formative experience Mary developed not only an appreciation of the need to communicate effectively with children about sexual matters, but also the skills to do so with appropriate sensitivity – recognising that not to do so would amount to adding to the child's distress, not alleviating it, and therefore constituting further abuse, albeit unintentionally. As Fahlberg (1981), another pioneer in the child care field, argued at around this time, the very fact that adults hesitate to share information about the past with a child implies to that child that their past is so bad that they will not be able to cope with it. Whatever the past may have been, they had the resilience to live through it and survive, enabling them to live with the truth.

A key part of this communication with traumatised children was the development of the 'toy box'. The toy box approach has been a significant contributor to the development of effective ways of relating to children and helping them to talk about highly sensitive, confusing and painful memories of abusive experiences. It involves using specially created or adapted toys (anatomically correct dolls, for example) to provide a vehicle for young children to communicate about their experiences. Simply talking to children without any such aids is likely to be far less effective in gathering the necessary information to form the basis of an assessment. The toys provide a focal point for not only sharing information, but also for developing a relationship based on trust – something that can otherwise be very difficult with children whose trust has been abused in the process of being sexually or otherwise abused.

Key point

Effective communication is at the heart of trauma recovery: communication with the child in age-appropriate ways, plus communication with the other professionals involved in the recovery process. Everyday communication skills are a good start, but these will generally not be enough on their own. It is essential for anyone working with traumatised children to develop their communication skills to a more advanced level over time.

Practice focus 1.1

I used to go and see a young woman in a children's home. The other children were quite used to me arriving with various pieces of play equipment. There was a young man who had been removed from home because both parents were drug abusers and there was concern that he was being sexually abused, although he had never said anything. He met me in the hall. 'What have you brought today?' I told him about the smiling doll, which, if you opened a flap on his chest and looked in his heart, you could see another little doll who was crying. He said: 'Oh yes, I know all about that'. If I had had permission to work with him, that would have been the moment. Sadly, I didn't.

What was also important about this phase in Mary's career was that it enabled her to draw on her own experiences of rejection and shame in making a meaningful connection with the children she was trying to help – a connection without which little progress was likely to be made. This highlights what was to emerge as a key principle: the need to 'tune in' to the child's experiences of hurt and harm and not simply assume that, once the abuse was over, things would steadily return to normal.

The ability to think outside the box, to use creative opportunities in direct work and to place the child's best interest at the centre of thinking and practice – all core elements of effective practice – evolved from Mary's experiences and became part and parcel of the approach she and her colleagues adopted.

The recognition of sexual abuse as a significant social phenomenon had a wide social impact. It occurred at the time of increased awareness of gender inequality. This emerging realisation led to the recognition that powerful, evil men were sexually abusing some adolescent girls. The thinking at the time was very much about powerful men doing evil things to teenage girls, and it was not until the early 1980s that society began to understand that it was not only adolescent girls, it was young girls – and sometimes even babies too – who were being abused by these same powerful, evil men. The sexual abuse of boys by men was also becoming more widely recognised. In the early 1990s it became clear that women could also sexually abuse children. Before this recognition took root, it was difficult to suggest that women could be abusers – the very idea would have attracted criticism, if not ridicule. It took a long time for the thinking and the policy to catch up with what was being seen by Mary and her team in practice.

Whatever it was that was stopping people talking about sexual abuse before was now starting to give way to a much stronger emphasis on sexual abuse. Whatever communication between professionals and the child that stood in the way of disclosure about what was happening was having to change. Whatever was stopping adolescents telling us about what was happening to them started to fade when things changed the late 1970s. Similarly, whatever was stopping younger girls and boys telling us about abuse began to recede in the 1980s, as did whatever was stopping children telling us what their mothers did to them in the 1990s. Whether it was professionals putting up barriers so these children could not be heard or other causes (or some such combination) remains unclear and probably always will. However, what is certain is that over time the climate around disclosure of abuse has changed in major ways.

From this, what gradually became apparent was that sexual abuse was much more common than had originally been thought, and was not purely a matter of certain men creating opportunities to have sex with underage girls (abhorrent though that was). It gradually dawned on the professionals involved that they were dealing with much more of a viper's nest of abuse, also involving pre-adolescent girls, boys and babies, with both male and female perpetrators from across the social spectrum. This was a much bigger and much more complex social problem than anyone had realised, and Mary found herself at the centre of efforts to tackle the many challenges involved. Her sensitivity to children's pain made her well placed to respond effectively to these challenges.

Recognising the significance of trauma

What also proved to be very significant about the emerging experience of working with sexually abused children was the recognition of the *traumatic* impact of abuse; the awareness that the abuse was not only problematic in itself, but also left the child or young person with a form of psychological wound. Although the term 'trauma' was not one that was commonly used at that time, we can now see that trauma, as currently conceptualised, was exactly what so many children were experiencing as a result of the abuse they had suffered.

This recognition was to prove a key factor in the development of an innovative approach based primarily on the understanding of the need to address trauma in the lives of sexually abused children. In 1987, Mary began a journey which culminated in the provision of the country's leading specialist therapeutic centre for traumatised children. We shall return to this point below.

Mary's work has played an important part in the development of our awareness of abuse-related trauma and its impact alongside other developments (for example, in neuropsychology), which have not only emphasised the importance of understanding trauma, but also provided a platform for developing our practice responses to the challenges involved. The remainder of this chapter focuses on important aspects of how the knowledge base underpinning the Mary Walsh Approach casts light on trauma and recovery, beginning with a discussion of four core beliefs.

Four core beliefs

The approach is underpinned by four core beliefs that have informed the work of Mary and her colleagues throughout. These beliefs form important value statements that are worth exploring to demonstrate their significance. We will examine each in turn:

1. Children come first

Being child centred is a longstanding value proposition in children's services (Barnes, 2018). Adult support and protection are important, but if this is not balanced by a commitment to being child centred, then there is a danger that adult concerns and issues take precedence over the children's issues. This is fundamentally a power issue in the sense that adults, for the most part, are in more powerful positions than children and so, unless efforts are made to address this imbalance, what will routinely happen is that the voices of adults will be heard but the voices of children will not. The traditional idea that children should be seen and not heard is given little credence these days, but it remains the case that there is a very real danger that children's needs and concerns will be drowned out by the needs and interests of adults. The need to be child centred is so pronounced that we devote a whole chapter to the issues involved (Chapter 6).

Child-centred practice is important for any child, but for an abused child, where they may have been exposed to harm and subsequent trauma, their trust in adults is likely to have been eroded through the actions of adults who have had care of them. As we shall see, abused children are – understandably, given the severe breaches of trust they will have experienced – likely to have difficulty in trusting people. Rebuilding trust is an important part of helping children recover from the trauma of abuse, and giving them the message that we are taking them and their concerns seriously is an important element of that. Trust is vitally important because: (i) we are unlikely to get very far in helping a child to recover if they do not trust us; and (ii) it is important for children to learn to trust again, as facing adult life without a basis of trust is likely to lead to considerable difficulties and privations, with possible adverse consequences for their mental health.

The introduction of the Children Act 1989 reflected the longstanding value in children's social care that the child's needs are paramount. It is easy to see that, in the same way, child-centred practice adopts the same recognition. Good practice therefore requires us to place the child at the centre of our concerns and not allow adult issues to take precedence. Within the environment of therapeutic childcare, this need to be child centred is constantly under threat from the potentially competing needs of adults, whether parents, therapeutic parents or any other party responsible for the well-being and care of abused children.

2. Listening to children

Children communicate in different ways, and so it is important that we become attuned to these so that we can connect meaningfully with the children we are trying to help. Children who have been sexually abused have had their own needs suppressed by an adult who has prioritised their own sexual desires over the child's well-being. Listening effectively to children is a skilled undertaking, but the time and effort it takes to learn these skills are certainly worthwhile.

For example, as we indicated above, it is very easy for the voice of the child not to be heard if there are (more powerful) adults around having their say. This can result in an adverse effect on self-esteem and can discourage children from speaking up if they learn that it is pointless to do so because they are being drowned out by the voices of adults and their agendas.

Putting children first and listening to them are therefore central considerations, as we shall explore in more detail in Chapter 6.

3. Helping children heal

The assumption that children will simply 'get over' abuse once they are removed from an abusive situation has proven to be wrong, and dangerously so, leaving many children and adults to handle some very painful and distressing (if not actually traumatic) situations. The need to *recover* from abuse is a key feature of the Mary Walsh Approach. 'Healing', in a spiritual, whole-person – rather than purely bodily – sense is a key part of this (we return to the subject of spirituality below). As we shall explore in more detail, it is helpful to think of trauma as the emotional and spiritual equivalent of a wound or injury. The idea of 'healing' can therefore be understood as a basic part of the process of recovery, by the same analogy.

There is much to be gained from giving children the opportunity to establish a sense of having moved on and an ability to understand their past, putting it into the perspective of their life and their past abuse not having any power over how they feel and how they think. This is unlikely to happen spontaneously, but it can be facilitated by skilled and committed people who are well informed about the issues involved. It is, as we mentioned earlier, a process of transformation from victim to survivor.

There is no formulaic approach to helping children heal, but there are patterns to be aware of and helpful steps that can be taken, and these have formed a major part of the underpinning philosophy. It is not a matter of 'warehousing' children, as that could potentially create more problems than it solves. It is a matter of helping children to recover, to move on in their lives, and to leave the pain behind. In order to assist children in developing the courage to move on in their lives it is essential to have an attachment to one or more significant persons to help them with such a painful process. This needs to be a significant relationship with one or more people who are there with them, walking alongside them as they recover (see the discussion of the 'fellow traveller' in Holloway and Moss, 2010).

4. Working with sexual abuse is important

The fact that so many children are subjected to sexual abuse is in itself an outrage. Significant sums of money are rightly invested in trying to prevent such abuse from taking place or, at the very least, for it to be detected in the early stages to keep the harm to a minimum. However, there is a strong argument that much more needs to be done to help deal with the aftermath of such abuse. This is because, as we shall see in Chapter 4, the effects of abuse can be devastating for young lives and can blight health, development and well-being (Rogers & Pilgrim, 2014). We therefore need to make sure that we do not lose sight of how significant a social problem sexual abuse is and how profoundly detrimental its effects can be (Thompson, 2017b). The term 'child sexual abuse' can easily be bandied about to the point where it loses its potency, where the acute pain and suffering and the immense destruction involved become sanitised, watered down by repeated routine use. For example, both of the present authors have come across situations where people have been joking about sexual abuse in a way that suggests they were either unaware of, or insensitive to, the immense harm such abuse causes (see Chapter 4).

We need to make sure that we do not lose sight of the fact that the idea of child abuse can so easily become dissociated from a child being prodded or poked or suffocated – in essence, from the reality of a child's pain. 'Child sexual abuse', especially when abbreviated to CSE, can become just words that we use, a label that has become disconnected from the horrific experiences involved. In a very real sense, such usage can represent a denial of the child's reality. This may be understandable in terms of professionals wanting to insulate themselves from all that pain for their own protection and self-care needs, but it is nonetheless a dangerous and potentially harmful path to go down (the issue of self-care is one we shall revisit in Chapter 8).

Similarly, the tendency to 'water down' the impact of trauma by using the term very loosely to refer to any distressing situation, including ones that are far from traumatic, distances us from the enormity of the harm associated with actual trauma.

Clearly, we have to find ways of ensuring that we do not in any way lose sight of the child's reality. Not only is this a key practice principle if we want our efforts to help to be effective, but it is also a *value* statement, in the sense that it both reflects and encapsulates a genuine commitment to addressing a major social evil.

Figure 1.1: Four core beliefs

1. Children come first

2. Listening to children

3. Helping children heal

4. Working with sexual abuse is important

Key point

These four core beliefs serve as important practice principles. They are not the only issues to be borne in mind, of course, but experience has taught us that if we neglect one or more of these principles we significantly reduce our capacity to make a positive difference and can actually find ourselves in situations where we are doing harm or reinforcing harm that has already been done.

Making a difference: The starfish story

Effective practice in relation to trauma recovery requires a strong commitment to making a positive difference. The work involved is not for the faint hearted. That commitment has been evidenced by those involved in developing the Mary Walsh Approach, and it has never wavered, despite many obstacles (as we shall see in Chapter 2), even though the sheer extent of the problem can appear overwhelming at times. What is needed is a degree of determination and persistence and the recognition that, while we cannot solve the overall problem of sexual abuse, nor make sure that every child who is abused receives the help and support they need, we can make a difference to some children's lives – and that is a very worthwhile endeavour indeed.

A key term here is 'humility', in the sense of being able to recognise the limitations of what we can realistically achieve, without allowing those limitations to discourage or detract us. It is essential to get the balance right. The fact that we cannot help every child should not be misinterpreted that we cannot help *any* child. Similarly, the fact that we will not succeed with all the children we try to help does not mean we will not succeed with any. The huge extent and massive impact of the problem is not a reason for not doing whatever we reasonably can to make a positive difference.

Many people will be familiar with the story of the starfish, a story that nicely illustrates the importance of humility and a willingness to do our best, despite what seem like the huge odds against us. Loren Eiseley once wrote a short tale of hope (Eiseley, 1969). The day after a big storm a man was walking on the beach and saw a boy picking up something and very gently throwing it into the ocean.

As he got closer, he called out, 'What are you doing?' The boy paused, looked up and replied: 'Throwing starfish into the ocean'.

'Why are you throwing starfish into the ocean?' asked the man.

The boy said, 'The tide is going out, and if I don't throw them in, they'll die'.

The man stated, 'There are thousands of starfish on this beach. You can't possibly make a difference!' The boy listened politely, then bent down and picked up another starfish. He then threw it into the sea, past the breaking waves: 'It made a difference for that one!'

Later that afternoon, the man realised that he had missed out on the essential nature of the boy's actions. He realised that what the boy was doing was choosing not to be an observer, but to intervene. When the morning came he awoke knowing that he had to do something. He got up, put on his clothes, went to the beach and found the boy. And, with him, he spent the rest of the morning throwing starfish into the ocean.

This is an important message, as both of the present authors have come across people who have thought of giving up their work in trauma recovery, or in child protection more broadly, because they felt weighed down by the enormity of the problem, the quantity (the sheer numbers of children involved), the quality (the intensity of the horrific harm done) and the duration (childhood trauma can have lifelong detrimental effects, often highly disabling effects, as we shall see in Chapter 4).

> **Practice focus 1.2**
>
> Peggy was a little girl who came to live with us when she was very young. She was very disturbed as a result of her extended abuse at the hands of her violent father, and it took a long time before she felt safe and calm enough to settle. After four years of intensive work with her she was ready to think about going to live with an alternative family. At one of the children's parties she came and sat on my knee and whispered in my ear: 'Thank you for saving my life'.

Sadly, complete success in tackling child abuse and the traumas it brings is likely to elude us. However, we should not allow that to distract us from the fact that there is much we can do to prevent abuse from ruining at least some children's lives. The starfish story can serve to remind us of this crucial fact, especially at those times when we are struggling to make progress and need to hold on to the hope that we can indeed make a significant difference. None of us can rescue everybody, but we can all make the difference to one child.

It is understandable that it can easily be the case that we can feel overwhelmed by the enormity of the task in working with abuse, but this means that our ability to hold on to the importance of getting it right for that particular child is paramount. This has self-care and staff support implications, and so we shall return to this point in Chapter 8.

Communicating with children

The importance of communicating with traumatised children has been a central plank in developing the quality of practice needed to bring out positive outcomes for them. There is a long tradition of 'direct work' with children (Tait & Wosu, 2013) which emphasises the importance of play as a form of communication. As we noted earlier, Mary's contribution to the development of this tradition has been her pioneering work in the use of toys as aids to communication. Her 'toy box' approach has been a significant contributor to the development of effective ways of relating to children who, due to a combination of developmental level, low levels of trust (caused by abuse) and the highly sensitive, confusing and painful nature of the subject matter, are likely to struggle with straightforward conversation. The toy box approach provides a non-threatening way of creating opportunities for children to express their feelings, convey difficult and extremely sensitive information and – just as importantly – to feel listened to, validated and thus valued.

A further important aspect of communication (with adults and children) is the use of humour. This too is an important feature of the Mary Walsh Approach. Those who have worked with Mary over the years will confirm that she has shown – and supported in others – the use of humour as a means of facilitating communication and positive relationships. It can also be used as a way of coping with the inevitable pressures that arise. In this way humour can be used positively as a helpful coping method or negatively as a form of avoidance behaviour (that is, as a form of escapism that tries to deny the reality of the situation). Clearly, the positive use of humour has much to commend it, whereas the latter presents significant dangers.

Communication is fundamental to how we relate to one another, whether adult to adult, adult to child, child to adult or child to child (Thompson, 2018a). Communicating with children goes above and beyond everyday communication skills for most of us, and there is much to be gained, as we indicated earlier, from taking our skills to a more advanced level, taking every opportunity to learn and develop – for example, not only by practising our skills directly, but also by watching how more experienced colleagues operate and of course from reading about the subject. But whichever method of learning (or combination of methods) is your preferred option, the need to build on our foundation of communications skills remains highly important.

Communication skills are also central to leadership, of course, and it is to that topic that we now turn.

Leadership

If we accept that to influence thinking and practice is a form of leadership, then clearly Mary merits the title of leader. She has not only led the country's leading therapeutic residential service through over a quarter of a century of successful practice, but also left a much broader imprint on therapeutic work with sexually abused children (later extended to all trauma-related work).

Traditionally the hallmark of leadership has been seen as the ability to develop a vision of where the people concerned need to get to, the insight to forge a path to get there and the skills of gaining the credibility needed for followers to be committed to being part of the journey (Thompson, 2016a). This is also part of the Mary Walsh Approach, in so far as Mary's own work has exemplified the importance and value of having a clear vision (rooted in the four core beliefs discussed earlier in this chapter) and being able to support and inspire people in pursuing that vision.

This vision has laid the foundations for the broad influence Mary's work has had, not least in terms of:

- *Addressing abuse-related trauma:* This in itself is a significant step forward, as the traditional, but seriously flawed idea that the effects of trauma will wither away once its causes have been removed remains influential. Despite the strong challenges to this unhelpful assumption, it has not been eradicated altogether; far from it, in fact. So, while good progress has been made, there is still work to be done to put this false assumption to bed once and for all.

- *Developing a three-factor approach to abuse-related trauma to deliver recovery for children:* The combination of individual therapy, therapeutic parenting and life story work has been a mainstay of the success of the Mary Walsh Approach in helping children to recover from their trauma. It has been a refreshing validation of this approach when viewing replicated work across the UK. This has been based on Mary's approach and underpinned by her desire to share this practice through the publication of the SACCS book series (see the *Guide to further learning* on p183). We shall revisit this three-factor model in more detail below.

- *The use of the toy box technique:* Mary's use of a toy box for communicating with abused children has been an important development. While others had used such techniques with children in other contexts, Mary was among the first to use this method with sexually abused children, first as an investigative tool and later as a process to provide safety and confidence for children to tell their stories.

Another leadership characteristic is the ability to remain focused and committed in the face of immense difficulties, and this too is certainly part of Mary's experience. In the early days of her work she faced a number of obstacles that she and her team had to surmount. These obstacles included:

- The resistance from neighbours to the first house that was established as a residential base for abused children – a sad example of the NIMBY (Not in My Back Yard) phenomenon.

- The adverse media attention that plagued Mary and her team in the early years of SACCS. Mary had been asked to give evidence in court. Her evidence spoke of the abuse revealed by the children. However, the judge rejected this in favour of the parents' evidence which had been, in his own words, 'given with dignity'. A major newspaper became aware of this and portrayed Mary as someone who received payment for making children present a false impression of what had happened to them. Fortunately, Mary had sufficient courage in her own convictions (another leadership quality), as well as support from others in the profession, to be able work through this difficult and painful experience and continue to invest in giving children a voice. At this time, children were rarely given credence in court proceedings; for those that were practicing at this time, the introduction of the Memorandum of Good Practice on Video Recorded Interviews with Child Witnesses was just being introduced.

■ A situation where, for child-centred reasons, one of the SACCS houses went over its maximum number of children as specified in its registration conditions for a few days. This resulted in the local authority taking SACCS to court. Fortunately, this time the judge was more understanding of a child's needs and concerns and found in SACCS's favour, recognising that a technical breach of the regulations for a short period of time was far less of an issue than providing a safe haven for an abused child in an emergency situation. So, although this was a positive outcome, it had proven to be a very challenging and stressful experience.

These are just some of the setbacks and challenges that could have derailed the SACCS project, but did not do so due to the commitment of Mary and her team.

One final aspect of leadership that we want to comment on is that of the ability to shape workplace cultures in a positive direction. Organisational cultures are very powerful and can be positive or negative in their influence. The ability to shape the culture in a positive direction is therefore an important element of leadership (Thompson, 2016a).

Key point

Mary's work has exemplified leadership in a number of ways. However, we should not confuse leadership with management. It is reasonable to expect any child care professional, whether a manager or not, to evidence leadership in order to achieve the best outcomes for traumatised children, in the form of a principled commitment to children that has the potency to succeed, despite the obstacles, setbacks and challenges involved.

A spiritual approach

For many people, spirituality automatically equates with religion. However, as Moss (2005) explains, religion is a very important form of spirituality, but it is not the only one. Spirituality is a matter of finding meaning and purpose in life, of having a sense of who we are and how we fit into the wider world, what matters to us and what does not, who and what we feel connected to and how all this shapes our outlook or worldview (*Weltanschauung*, to use the philosophical term).

Trauma can be recognised as a spiritual issue, in the sense that it seriously challenges, if not completely devastates, our spirituality, our sense of who we are, what is safe, what is meaningful, and how we relate to other people (Sangster & Lee, 2017; Walsh & Thompson, 2017). Indeed, Thompson (2012), in his discussion of the significance of loss and grief in people's lives, argues that loss and grief challenge our ability to cope; crisis overwhelms our ability to cope and trauma devastates our ability to cope. This sense of devastation is precisely what makes childhood trauma so destructive for everyone, but especially for children who will have had little or no experiences of learning from adversity to draw upon.

We can therefore understand trauma as a form of spiritual diminishment, as an undermining of our being. It is for this reason that psychological trauma is often referred to as an existential trauma, to indicate that it has spiritual as well as emotional consequences (Thompson & Walsh, 2010).

Spirituality is also about awe, wonder and beauty, and it needs to be recognised that trauma can often prevent people from appreciating these things, or even recognising that they exist. This is part of trauma that can lead to a sense of no longer being a whole person, of being in some way 'diminished' by the experience:

'Children traumatised by serious abuse or profound neglect have suffered harm to their person, their innocence, their emotional and their spiritual well-being, and the right to grow up in their own families. Because these injuries are so profound they affect both their external and internal worlds.'
(Walsh, 2009, p9)

In a sense, adopting a spiritual understanding of trauma has been another dimension of the Mary Walsh Approach. The spiritual or existential aspects of trauma have received relatively little attention in the mainstream literature or in traditional professional practice (Thompson & Walsh, 2010; Thompson, 2017c). However, it is an important element of the approach and will therefore feature in later chapters at appropriate points.

Making an impact

The values underpinning the Mary Walsh Approach led to SACCS having the reputation of an organisation that 'punches above its weight', in the sense that, for a relatively small team, it has had a significant influence on the development of theory and practice in the field of abuse-related childhood trauma. Mary and some of her colleagues have been speakers at prestigious conferences around the world; have provided training and consultancy for a wide range of organisations, and produced a well-received series of books on childhood trauma (see the *Guide to further learning* on p183). Mary has also been instrumental in developing an innovative foundation degree in therapeutic childcare at one university and a Master's programme at another. These developments indicate how the situation has evolved over the years, from the early days when little or nothing was known about the issues involved, to being able to study the subject at Master's level.

Of course, it is not expected that everyone working with children who have been abused will need to study the subject matter at an advanced level, but it does mean that there is a significant knowledge base there for us to work from. From that knowledge base we are able to identify six key themes, and so it is worth exploring each of these in turn in order to appreciate their significance.

Key point

Childhood trauma is a vast and complex area of study, and so there is always more that we can learn to become better equipped to respond positively to abused children's needs. We should never make the assumption that we have reached the point where there is nothing left to learn.

Six themes

The Mary Walsh Approach has helped thousands of children to recover from trauma. Underpinning this work have been six recurring themes; six key messages that have run throughout the work of Mary and her team over the years. By highlighting these here we are playing a part in laying down foundations to support future work and development.

1. We can make a difference

The intense reactions of children to abuse can be so shocking as to leave us feeling hopeless and helpless in terms of being able to do anything positive. For example, encountering a seven-year old girl using highly sexualised language can be a very disorientating experience. Similarly, the disturbed and disturbing behaviour displayed by traumatised children can easily lead to a sense of despair, a feeling that nothing could possibly undo the harm done that has produced such grotesque results at the expense of a child's innocence. However, it is vitally important that we do not lose hope; that we are able to hold on to the idea that there is indeed much we can do to help children move beyond their trauma and to achieve some degree of recovery.

Part of this is the recognition that setbacks are to be expected. The route of progression will not always go directly forward. Two steps forward, one step back is a common pattern. Sometimes there can be so many setbacks that it is understandable that we might feel that we are not getting anywhere. However, we have to make sure that we do not allow such difficulties to lead us to give up on the child or children concerned. Consider for a moment the implications of giving up on a child. What difference would it have made to your life if someone involved in your care and development had given up on you?

2. Sexual abuse is not a life sentence

While the trauma associated with abuse can have profoundly detrimental effects on a long-term basis, it does not mean that there is no way out of the hell this can bring. With the knowledge we have developed (and must continue to develop), the skills that have been honed and the value commitment to making a positive difference to the lives of abused children, we can make a significant contribution. While traumatised children can be helped to begin their journey of recovery, it is by no means certain that any child will recover completely from their ordeal. It is abundantly clear that very many children have been helped and very many more will continue to be helped as a result of the foundational work that has been set down, but complete success is never guaranteed.

While the impact of sexual abuse (and, indeed, other forms of abuse) can be major and long term if not properly addressed, it is possible for children and young people to make the transition we mentioned earlier, namely from victim to survivor. There is a process of healing and recovery that can be facilitated to enable the trauma to be dealt with and to leave the child or young person concerned free to get on with their life without being dominated by the psychological harm that trauma beings.

3. Attachment issues are central

Infants are, of course, extremely vulnerable, as they are not able to look after themselves. They rely heavily on one or more adults to keep them safe, to nurture them and to meet the needs that they are not yet able to meet for themselves. They therefore need to form close bonds with one or more reliable and protective adults. Such attachments then become the basis not only of their physical safety, but also of their emotional security (Howe, 2005). It is through attachments that the child learns to trust adults. Tragically, sexual abuse on the part of a parent or carer involves betraying that trust by forcing (physically or emotionally) a child to engage in a sexual relationship that they are not ready for. To be abused by any adult is detrimental enough, but to be abused by someone you trust and rely upon is significantly worse, heightening the sense of vulnerability and insecurity.

Sex between mature adults is about a consenting, mutual relationship, which is intended to be pleasurable and of benefit for both parties. When we are talking about sexual abuse, it is a matter of one person exploiting another for his or her own purposes, and it is not intended to be mutual or reciprocal (although the abuser may fantasise that it is). And so what can easily happen is that, particularly a young child who is forced into that relationship then feels the need to please the abuser. In such manipulative, one-sided relationships, the children involved are likely to be encouraged to want to keep that person happy, to please them. Sexual abuse is therefore not only an intimate abuse of a child's body, it is also an abuse of trust – an abuse of an attachment a child has formed. Indeed, this is the basis of, and rationale for, grooming of potential victims. For some abusers, the development of an attachment is a normal, natural and healthy process that subsequently becomes abused, for example when an adult with no initial intention to abuse subsequently determines to do so, to take advantage of the trust that has built up. However, there will be others who have deliberately set out to form an attachment so that the trust developed by it can form the basis of an abusive and exploitative relationship. This is where grooming comes into the picture; it is where there has been a deliberate process of exploitation built on attachment and trust. This insidiousness is what makes it all the more contemptible, but also all the more harmful for the child who is not only exploited, but also has their trust destroyed, leaving them vulnerable to a range of emotional difficulties and thus obstacles to a fulfilling life.

4. Abuse is shrouded in secrecy and denial

There are aspects of life that society does not like to face up to, and child abuse can certainly be included in their number. Thompson (2015) makes the point that much of what happens in social work deals with aspects of our society that most people would prefer not to think about (or may not even know about), aspects that are considered shameful. Abuse of various kinds is part of this, including child abuse, where the extent and severity of the problem are not widely known to the general public. One of the consequences of this is there tends to be considerable secrecy and denial associated with such matters. This dynamic of denial can operate at different levels:

- **Individual**. In working directly with a child, issues of embarrassment, shame and stigma can create tension and stand in the way of open and productive communication. This can apply to child-adult conversations as well as adult-adult ones.

- **Familial**. Families will often play down worrying issues or signs. This is not restricted to abuse issues, of course. It will happen, for example, when health worries start to emerge. There will often be a tendency to hope for the best and push any worrying signs or symptoms to one side. This is dangerous enough when it happens in relation to health concerns, but can be extremely harmful when it applies to issues of abuse. Family members can find it extremely difficult to face up to the possibility that abuse is taking place, and so the pressure to rely on denial can be very strong.

- **Organisational**. Focusing on procedures and targets and losing sight of the child's reality and their pain are sadly not uncommon features of highly pressurised workplaces. Much will also depend on an organisation's culture, as this is a very powerful influence on behaviour (Thompson, 2016a). Cultures are basically a set of habits, taken-for-granted assumptions and unquestioned assumptions, and this is what gives them their power – they influence people without their realising, because members of the organisation come to accept the culture as the norm, as the basic reality in which they work. Where the culture is a procedures-centred one, rather than a child-centred one, secrecy and denial can be very much to the fore.

- **Societal**. While child abuse is very much a personal problem for those concerned, it is also a social problem, in the sense that its roots are very much in wider society in a number of ways (Thompson, 2017b). For example, social attitudes towards sexuality, children's less than full status as citizens and relative powerlessness, and sexism can all be significant elements of abuse scenarios. In addition, there is a tendency for the media to present child abuse as an aberrant pathology rooted in individual behaviour, rather than as a widespread social problem that reflects a complex and evolving interaction of personal and social factors. In a similar vein, Ferguson (2004) refers to the 'marginality' of not only perpetrators of abuse, but also the children who have been abused, as both groups are pushed to the margins of society. Again, this reflects the tendency for those aspects of society considered shameful or stigmatised to be brushed under the carpet to a large extent.

Mary Walsh and her team have historically played a significant part in challenging this dynamic by putting the trauma associated with sexual abuse firmly on the agenda for child care professionals. However, it is important to recognise that the painful and disturbing nature of child abuse – sexual abuse in particular – can easily seduce us into losing sight of the very harsh reality of abuse and trauma.

5. We must listen to children

As we have already noted, the need to listen to children is a key part of the Mary Walsh Approach, and so, in Chapter 6 we will explore in more detail what this entails. But, for now, we want to emphasise two particular points: (i) the importance of listening when abuse is known or suspected; and (ii) the danger of not picking up on abuse issues because we are not sufficiently 'tuned in' to the prevalence of abuse.

In terms of the first of these two points, it cannot be emphasised enough that effective work of any kind with children needs to be premised on a willingness and ability to listen. But when it comes to abused and traumatised children who have had their trust destroyed and been left to feel extremely vulnerable, its importance increases manifold. In effect, there is a very real danger that we will add to the child's sense of mistrust if we are not able or prepared to listen effectively.

In terms of the second of these two points, we should note that we continue to have a problem with the recognition of abuse as a deeply ingrained and widespread feature of life. Child abuse was not 'discovered' until the 1960s, in the sense that it was assumed before that time that parents could not harm their own children (but see Ferguson (2011) for a discussion of the more complex historical realities involved). It was not until the 1980s and the 'Cleveland affair' (in which large numbers of children were removed from their families on the basis of a medical test which was deemed sufficient to confirm that they had been sexually abused – see Bell (1988) and Campbell (1988) for conflicting views on this) that it started to be recognised that children, even very young children, could be sexually abused. We can speculate about why it took so long for us to become aware of such horrific practices that we now know had been going on long before they were 'discovered'. Part of that speculation can, of course, be the previous failure to listen to children, to take their concerns seriously or to create safe environments where children could make their concerns known.

More recently, the scandals associated with celebrity figures such as Jimmy Savile and Stuart Hall have now played a part in making the general public more aware of the extent of abuse, but unfortunately it is very easy for the actions of such powerful individuals to be seen as exceptions, as features of the distorted world of 'showbiz' and celebrity, largely disconnected from the everyday realities of ordinary life.

The concerns about abuse on the part of trusted figures in the Catholic Church, widely reported in the media, have also helped to raise awareness, but, again, it is very easy for these to be dismissed as exceptions, as reflections of a group of people in a limited and distinctive sector of society and therefore not recognised as part of the everyday realities of ordinary life either.

Furthermore, the concerns about young footballers being abused by coaches and others in powerful positions within professional football clubs, people who could ruin their career hopes if exposed as abusers, have also been widely publicised. But, yet again, these circumstances relate to a very small sector of society (people involved in professional football), and so, once again, it is very easy for these concerns to be disconnected from the everyday realities of ordinary life.

What these three contemporary examples highlight is that, despite the very significant concerns about the welfare and safety of children and young people, there is still a very strong tendency for child abuse to be seen as something divorced from mainstream society and social life – despite the statistics showing that abuse is far more commonplace than people generally realise (even some people who work every day with children).

The failure to be attuned to the extent of child abuse means that the 'signals' or 'messages' that children may be giving off are likely to be missed. For example, if someone approaches their interactions with a child with the mindset that abuse is a very rare occurrence, then important signals the child is giving off may be misinterpreted or missed altogether. We have already noted that abuse is an embarrassing and shameful matter, and so it is understandable that children who have been abused will be reluctant to make it known that they are indeed being abused. It takes a great deal of courage to disclose abuse, not least because of the potential major repercussions of doing so, especially for someone who is feeling vulnerable and unsafe. What will often happen, therefore, is that the child will give indirect messages that they are being abused. This may be in the form of drawings or other artwork, in the form of hints or through the things they don't actually say – the telling silences at times.

If, however, we are attuned to such matters and we have not shut down our observational faculties by filtering out the possibility of abuse, we are much more likely to pick up subtle cues and therefore be much more effective at listening to the messages that children are giving us.

Of course, it is important to get the balance right. We must not go to the opposite extreme and start over-reacting. It is very easy to become risk averse and thereby adopt an over-cautious approach.

6. We must care for the carers

Fundamentally, we cannot expect child care staff to function effectively if they are stressed, overloaded or unsupported in dealing with the emotional challenges of the work. It is therefore essential, if we are to make sure that children are properly cared for, that staff and foster carers are also properly cared for. The notion of 'workplace well-being' as a basic part of effective people management in any organisation has quite rightly received a great deal of attention over the years (Thompson, 2013). However, in workplaces that involve such emotionally challenging work as trauma recovery with abused children, it is an essential requirement for safe practice.

A key concept here is that of emotional 'holding' (Weld, 2009), also often referred to as containment. It refers to the need to provide an atmosphere where people (children or adults) have a sense of security, where they feel safe to be themselves. Employing organisations can play a part in providing 'holding' for their staff as part of a commitment to workplace well-being (Hesketh & Cooper, 2019; Thompson & Bates, 2009) – it is an important element of caring for the carers.

Once again it is a matter of organisational culture. Is the culture an open, responsive and supportive one or is it closed, unresponsive and unsupportive – an 'if you can't stand the heat, get out of the kitchen' type of macho culture? The answer to this question can make all the difference in terms of the quality of care (for children and staff). This brings us back to the topic of leadership and the need to shape and sustain a positive culture that helps rather than hinders.

The Mary Walsh Approach to this is encapsulated in the idea that it is very important that the children develop positive relationships with their carers. A great deal of energy invested in helping that happen is needed. For example, in residential care it is more important that the staff in the houses are able to contain children, that the managers are able to contain the staff and the senior management are able to contain everybody. Leadership involves a big responsibility in containing the whole, which can be very exhausting at times, hence the need for everyone to be supportive of everyone else.

This reflects the recognition that working with traumatised children is very demanding and potentially stressful work. Proper managerial and leadership safeguards therefore need to be put in place. Emotions are very powerful and, where not appropriately managed, can do a great deal of harm for all concerned.

Figure 1.2: Six themes

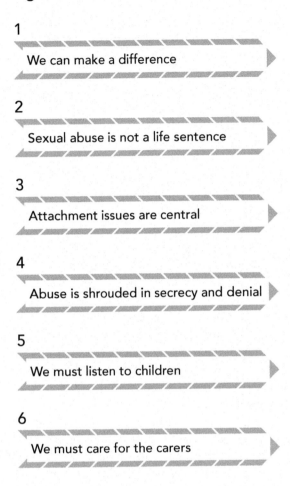

1

We can make a difference

2

Sexual abuse is not a life sentence

3

Attachment issues are central

4

Abuse is shrouded in secrecy and denial

5

We must listen to children

6

We must care for the carers

Conclusion

The Mary Walsh Approach has made a major contribution to our understanding of abuse-related childhood trauma (and helped thousands of children in the process), while also raising awareness of a hugely important set of issues that have traditionally been marginalised.

This chapter has reflected Mary's own journey, from her experiences as a child hurt by separation to a pioneer in making a positive difference in helping children traumatised by abuse. It has begun for us the process of mapping out how the key ideas have evolved and how they can be invaluable in practice. Chapter 2 continues this process.

Points to ponder

1. What does it mean to say that a child has been 'traumatised' by abuse?

2. The importance of listening to children has been emphasised. What harm might be done if we do not listen to children?

3. What might the consequences be for staff and/or foster carers if they are not given adequate support in dealing with these emotionally challenging issues?

Exercise

The point has been made that child abuse is much more widespread than people generally realise. What reasons do you think there are for the level of awareness not being much greater? What could possibly be done to improve the level of public and professional awareness?

Chapter 2: Developing the approach

Introduction

This chapter builds on the story told in Chapter 1 by discussing further how the ideas that underpin the Mary Walsh Approach developed and came to offer a comprehensive approach to helping abused children recover from their traumatic experiences. We follow the same pattern of briefly reviewing the historical background before moving on to look more closely at how the approach can be used effectively in practice.

The situation evolves

In Chapter 1 we noted that Mary developed at an early stage in her career a strong commitment to working with children who had been sexually abused. At that time, the idea of sexual abuse was relatively new and there were few people who had any experience or expertise in dealing with such challenges. Mary had joined a special unit for dealing with child abuse, one of the first to be set up in the country. At the time of her joining, it was an all-male team, and so it quickly transpired that she tended to receive the sexual abuse cases. She therefore found herself in a situation whereby she quickly accumulated considerable experience in working with sexually abused children and as a result rapidly developed a significant knowledge base and set of skills.

Her dissatisfaction with how the system worked at that point led her to consider taking a different path, helping abused children in a different context. This was the embryo that developed into SACCS. Mary was interested in communicating with children using the toy box (see Chapter 1). Mary and Madge Bray were soon to team up to found SACCS, Sexual Abuse Childcare Consultancy Services, a private company that would specialise in responding to the aftermath of child sexual abuse.

The significance of this development was that the creation of an organisation around Mary's expertise led to a solid foundation for other professionals to learn from her knowledge, skills and values, and thereby make their own contribution to the recovery process.

It was a brave move for Mary to walk out of a safe local authority job, a highly unusual and risky thing to do at that time. One of the first tasks after doing so was to explore how the use of the toy box could be adapted to work with sexually abused children to help them to talk about what had happened to them, and to do so in a non-threatening way. SACCS was launched in January 1987 to build a foundation of training and services that would enable a large number of children to be helped, far more than Mary and Madge Bray could help on their own.

This decision proved to be highly effective, as SACCS was able not only to help many children directly, but also influence practice through training, consultancy and publishing. Prior to SACCS's arrival, there had been a great deal of anxiety about how to talk to children about sex, and so many social workers found themselves with cases where they were very anxious about what was happening. They felt they did not have the skills to talk effectively with children, and it soon became the case that the new SACCS organisation was asked to do a lot of this kind of work.

A further important part of the early work was assessment work for the courts. This was important work because it involved helping children to externalise their pain. Key people were seeing that children's behaviour would change as a result of the work being done. Consequently, the team were asked to do longer and longer pieces of work with children, to help them recover. This represented a significant shift: from short-term assessment work geared primarily towards assisting courts to make decisions, to much longer therapeutic work geared towards helping the children to deal with the aftermath of their abusive experiences. The foundations of the SACCS therapeutic approach were now in place.

Through doing this type of work it became apparent to the team that there were children – very young children, three-, four-, five-year-olds – who were either so disturbed or so eroticised by what had happened to them that they were unable to be accommodated in foster care. Indeed, foster carers who were not adequately prepared or trained or supported to work with sexually abused children had very demanding children thrust upon them, and they had little understanding of what they were encountering and very little insight into what to do. For example, someone who is not emotionally prepared for a three-year old who is constantly trying to get into their bra or pants, or to look at them in the bathroom or get into bed with them is likely to find it a very difficult situation to handle. As the SACCS experience over the years has shown, it is no exaggeration that a three-year old can behave in such a disturbing way. It would, of course, be hard enough to cope with such behaviour from a sexualised 13-year-old, but when it is a three-year old, the challenge is far greater, almost unimaginably so. It can challenge our sexuality to a very considerable extent, and, of course, many of the foster carers concerned – well-intentioned, good people – were not able to handle such situations, resulting in the placement breaking down. For most, it would be necessary to attribute the breakdown to other causes, because how could they admit that they could not cope with a three-year-old's sexuality? The whole idea of a three-year old being sexualised is a very difficult concept to grasp, and so it would be very difficult to admit that such a personal, intimate thing was at the heart of the problem.

Consequently, because these issues were never identified explicitly, the child would be moved on, into the next placement. Because of the secrecy and denial that have characterised sexual abuse over the years, the problem was not addressed; it was submerged. Because the matter was never raised, the same thing would happen again, and the child would be moved on again and again. As Mary has previously explained it: 'Too little account is taken of the emotional needs of children traumatised through abuse… This is one reason why so many placements break down' (p14, in Rymaszewska & Philpot, 2006).

Practice focus 2.1

I was asked to work with six children who had been removed because of suspected physical and sexual abuse. The older children were reluctant to say anything about what had happened. The two older boys, aged eight and six, had both been found being sexually aggressive with younger children at school. Sam was three-years old, but his foster carer said he was sexually acting out in play particularly with a toy medical kit.

I had some play sessions with him to make an assessment for the court. During those sessions the children's guardian (Guardian ad litem) was also present, Sam demonstrated highly sexualised and predatory behaviour, immobilising and tricking me so that he could have access to my body. The children eventually disclosed abuse, from both their father and their mother who had encouraged all the children from a very young age to stroke and rub intimate parts of her body for her pleasure.

I wrote a strong report urging the court to consider specialist therapy for Sam. The judge made the order, but the local authority did not act, instead placing him for adoption. That placement lasted two months and he then had several other placements which all failed because of his sexualised behaviour.

When he was seven, he was referred for specialised residential help, but by now he was very much more disturbed and difficult to help.

What would then emerge was a form of abuse in its own right, that of 'serial placements', with each new move bringing a range of losses that would rarely be recognised or addressed (Thompson, 2012). Eventually the child would be labelled as 'unfosterable' and therefore placed in residential care, alongside adolescents on remand. This then became an example of what has come to be known as 'system abuse' – that is, the abuse of children brought about as a side effect of the very system designed to safeguard them from harm. This highly problematic situation was causing considerable distress and further trauma for many children, as well as for many foster carers. For the children, this made recovery all the more difficult, and for some foster carers the experience was so difficult that it led them to give up fostering – thereby losing a valuable resource much needed by other children.

Key point

If the need for trauma recovery work is not recognised at an early stage, the result can be further abuse and traumatisation for the child and even a potentially traumatic experience for the foster carers.

This is not to say that residential care is necessarily problematic. Indeed, it has been a key part of SACCS's success that the team have created small, effective residential houses (avoiding the dehumanising term 'units' that has been widely used over the years) that have provided a safe haven for many children in small groups. It is important to recognise that not all children are well suited to fostering situations, and traumatised children can, in effect, traumatise foster carers (consider the example of the sexualised three-year old above). Mary captures the sad reality of this situation when she comments that:

'For these children, families are dangerous places where they may be hurt, used sexually or just ignored, and somehow they think it is their fault. It is not surprising, therefore, that when placed in another family they will often act out their beliefs in a frightening and destructive way – both for themselves and their alternative family – and another rejection will result.'
(p9, in Thomas & Philpot, 2009)

High-quality residential care can be the best solution for the right children in the right circumstances (Smith & Fulcher, 2013). While it is recognised that law and policy relating to child care are premised on the idea that children are best placed within their family, and, failing that, within a substitute family, it has to be recognised also that this is not the best option for some children. Residential settings with suitably trained, experienced and supported staff and an ethos and culture of therapeutic care can be a much more positive option for some children who mistrust family settings, which are where they were abused. However, much depends on the quality of assessment, being able to work out from knowing the child and their circumstances well which type of setting is likely to work best for them.

A conscious decision was made for the SACCS team to focus on working with young children. Mary resisted taking older children because she believed that children at SACCS need to have a strong relationship before the kind of florid adolescent behaviours appear, otherwise all that is happening is fire fighting, which is no substitute for being able to help children to recover. Consequently, the mission was to help children recover and to do that, what was needed was the development of really strong relationships, so that the children were able to feel that they could flourish and grow within that relationship. This became the basis of the model used within SACCS and by many other child care professionals influenced by SACCS training and publications.

The focus on younger children is particularly significant, in the sense that the younger the child is, the less likely they are to understand what is happening to them and therefore be able to 'process it' – that is, to make sense of it so that they are not so terrified by the painful and confusing things that are happening to them. For example, a 12-year-old who has been sexually abused knows they have been abused, they know that what has happened to them should not have taken place. However, a seven-year-old might know about sex, but not be aware that what is happening to them is about sex. It might be perceived by the child as 'rude' and therefore understood to be wrong. They would know it hurt and that it is frightening, but they would be fairly powerless in such a situation. For a two-year-old, however, it is a very different situation: they would not know it was about sex, nor would they know it was something 'rude'. But, because any sexual behaviour acted out on them by the abuser for their own sexual release squeezes the life out of them, they might very well feel that they nearly died.

This takes us back to the key issue of attachment. Not only is the child being abused, but, where the abuser is in a parental role, it can be understood as a form of 'double whammy', in the sense that, in addition to the abuse itself, there is the negative impact on the development of an attachment, thereby raising the trust issues that we discussed in Chapter 1. To put it metaphorically, not only is the child under attack, but they are also being denied the protection that they should be able to rely on.

> **Key point**
>
> Where the perpetrator is a parent or someone in a parental role, the abuse is likely to have an adverse effect on the child's attachment, with the likely consequence that the abused child finds it difficult to trust adults – even adults who are trying to help them recover from their trauma.

A key issue for SACCS has been to focus on the *abuse* element of sexual abuse. This is because sexuality is a perfectly natural thing in itself, but abuse arises in those situations where it involves people who are not able, because of their age or their developmental level, to deal with the emotional issues that are part and parcel of sexuality. What is likely to ensue, then, in such abusive situations, is that the child's sense of what relationships are all about becomes distorted. For example, if a child's father is also their sexual partner, then the ensuing distortion is clearly of major proportions. It is a distortion of both the parental relationship and of the sexual relationship. As such, it will cause all sorts of problems in view of the fact that the sexual abuse has been very painful and yet delivered by a person who has given them life and who is charged with their care, protection and nurturance.

Thompson and Walsh (2010) discuss the close links between being abused and feeling that you are dying. This is particularly relevant in cases of parental sexual abuse: if the child believes that they are being killed by a person that has given them life, the resulting confusion is likely to be immense and, frankly, some children will never recover from that experience.

It also has to be recognized that, while adults who are abused in later life may struggle with all the confusion and distortion that such an exploitative, manipulative relationship creates, at least they have some basis of pre-abuse normality with which to compare it, and some experience in recovering from situations of adversity. However, if we are talking about young children, then they will not have had the opportunity to form any strong sense of reality before that then gets distorted. They will then struggle to recognise it as a distortion and will have difficulty in trying to conceptualise the 'normality' that would take them away from the abuse – the abuse is their normality.

A key issue here is that of loss and grief. Grief is, by its very nature, a painful, frightening and exhausting experience and not something that we can just 'get over'. However, what we can do is learn from previous experiences of grief. For example, as adults we may well realise that although the grief is painful, the pain will subside over time (although it may never go away altogether). For children, especially young children, it is likely that they have not yet had chance to learn about loss and grief, and will therefore struggle even more with its challenges. This can make it all the more demanding and frightening.

With this in mind, it is important to recognise that trauma is a form of loss, a form of grief experience, albeit an extreme one (Thompson, 2017c). Consider, for example, the losses involved in being abused: trust, a sense of safety, self-respect, and many more. Young children who have not yet had chance to learn the lessons of loss are likely to be very ill-equipped to deal with the major emotional and spiritual challenges involved.

We say 'spiritual' because part of what loss and trauma challenge is our sense of self, our sense of who we are and how we fit into the wider world, how we find meaning and create a self-narrative that guides us through life's troubles. Children exposed to traumatic experiences will therefore face not only emotionally distressing losses, but also a form of spiritual diminishment, with significant obstacles to developing a sense of self characterised by self-respect and a high level of self-esteem. Harvey (2002) refers to trauma as an 'assault on the self', and this is a very apt term in general. However, it is particularly apt for young children who are in the very early stages of identity formation and whose life development can be seriously blown off course by such adverse experiences as abuse. We shall return later to the highly significant role of loss and grief in relation to trauma, but for now we should bear in mind that the younger the child, the less well equipped they are likely to be to withstand the assault on their embryonic sense of self.

Key point

To develop a fuller understanding of trauma and its immense impact on children who have been abused, it is essential to incorporate at least a basic knowledge of issues relating to loss and grief.

Clearly, then, Mary and her team at SACCS came to be involved in some extremely complex, incredibly challenging and highly sensitive work over a long period of time. There have, of course, been failures as well as successes along the way, but what is particularly important is that there has been learning throughout that period. That learning has been consolidated into a distinctive recovery programme – the Walsh Recovery Programme (WRP). We will be looking at this in some detail later in this chapter, but first we need to pursue further the rationale behind setting up SACCS in order to understand the key elements of thinking in their historical context.

Developing the Mary Walsh Approach

Basically, the Beatles were wrong: love is not all you need. As we have noted, the idea that abused children will naturally 'recover' from their ordeal if they are removed from the harmful circumstances and placed in a loving environment has proven to be far too optimistic. History has shown that significant problems are likely to emerge if steps are not taken to address the trauma provoked by the abuse. The work of SACCS has become part of that history by challenging the 'all you need is love' thesis.

It is as if the traditional approach had lost sight of what trauma actually means. Parallel with a physical trauma in the sense used by the medical profession, a trauma is an injury, a psychosocial and existential or spiritual injury (Walsh & Thompson, 2017). It is a major assumption that such injuries will heal effectively of their own accord without any form of therapeutic intervention. If we take the analogy of a broken leg, it may well heal unaided, eventually, but it is likely to be in a distorted way if the broken bone is not set properly, potentially leading to problems in walking thereafter throughout the person's life. Likewise, an abuse-related trauma can have an emotionally and spiritually distorting effect throughout the child's life if it is not 'set' properly through appropriate therapeutic recovery.

Key point

Just as a physical trauma that goes untreated will either not heal or will heal in a distorted and unhelpful way, a psychological trauma that is not addressed will either not heal or lead to a range of problems associated with emotional responses, trust and mental and spiritual well-being more broadly.

A key feature of the Mary Walsh Approach has therefore been an emphasis on the importance of recovery, which involves a process of addressing the hurt, confusion, disorientation, pain, suffering, distortion and undermining of self that characterise trauma. We will explore in more detail what this entails in Chapter 6. For now, however, we should note that the recognition of the need for recovery has been the foundation for the development of SACCS and the distinctive Mary Walsh Approach.

Part of that approach has been a willingness to be flexible and bring about change where necessary. This means that, while there is a tried and trusted approach that has been tested in practice over a 25-year period, it is not rigid or dogmatic, as that would distract attention from the need to focus on the child's needs. To get it right for the children is, of course, the basic aim. If the professionals involved are not getting it right, we have to be brave enough to say that something is not working; we must be willing to do things differently and research what differently means. As important as it is to be able to help people to understand what we are doing and give them some reassurance that what we are doing works, it needs to be clear that the limited financial resources available are being invested wisely. This is not simply about financial management; it is about making sure that we are able to help as many children as possible with the limited resources available.

The rationale behind setting up SACCS as an innovative organisation was therefore rooted in wanting to develop sophisticated ways of helping children recover from their abuse-related traumatic experiences and not make the naïve mistake of assuming that all they need is love.

The theoretical developments underpinning the Mary Walsh Approach have played an important role in raising awareness of the impact of trauma and in developing a structured but flexible approach to helping abused children recover from their traumatic experiences. It is to an explanation of that approach that we now turn.

The Walsh Recovery Programme

The approach that has evolved within SACCS has three core elements that are closely interrelated. This three-pronged approach comprises: individual therapy, life story work and therapeutic parenting. These are linked to a set of 24 outcomes which, when achieved, are indicative of the progress made – that is, they provide a framework for evaluating progress in a multidimensional way. Tomlinson and Philpot state that the approach is characterised by:

1. A commitment to pursuing 24 specific outcomes.

2. An assessment process comprising six key elements.

3. Three inter-related therapeutic modalities: individual therapy; life-story work; and therapeutic parenting.

4. A commitment to being child centred – as Walsh (2005) puts it: 'The journey to recovery is a long one and it belongs to the child. The child is at the centre of everything we do...'

(2008, p10).

We will return to the 24 outcomes and the six elements of assessment below. First, though, we need to be clear about what is involved in the three core elements of the programme to show the important part they play in helping the child to move forward.

Individual therapy

This involves developing an individually tailored programme of therapy geared towards promoting both recovery and resilience. It involves working at the child's pace and exploring key elements of their experience. The work is highly skilled and is rooted in a good understanding of child development, especially emotional development linked to attachment (Howe, 2005; Johnson, 2019). Some of the key theoretical concepts underpinning this work, such as attachment, will be explored in Chapter 3.

While individual therapy for abused children is by no means a new phenomenon, what is innovative in this approach is the recognition that such therapy is not enough on its own, that it needs to be part of a wider programme and fully integrated within that programme. It needs to be part of a holistic approach that takes account of wider issues, hence the three-pronged approach.

Often in the traditional approach, therapy happens in an exclusive situation. For example, where you might have a child being cared for by foster carers or in residential care, they go for, say, an hour a week to a therapist. What happens in that room is not known by anybody else; the child comes back, possibly has a bad reaction, the foster carers do not have a clue what has happened, may not be prepared for what might happen after therapy, and the child explodes or has some other reaction to what is happening in their head and the whole thing blows up and the placement can be ruined.

Traumatised children are very often 'split' internally, with conflicting sites of ideas and feelings, and such splitting can be extremely damaging. Individual therapy in isolation, unconnected with what else is going on in the child's care arrangements can contribute to such splitting, thereby potentially doing more harm than good. Consequently, a key feature of the Walsh Recovery Programme is the knitting together of the three elements, thereby avoiding the problem of therapy being disconnected from other important elements of the child's life.

In sum, then, individual therapy has a part to play, but it needs to be part of a holistic approach and not standalone.

Life story work

In tandem with individual therapy, the children served by SACCS are given the benefit of life story work. This has all the benefits of narrative therapy (an important concept that will be discussed in Chapter 3) which involves developing new structures of meaning. In an early work on the subject, Ryan and Walker capture some of the important points about how beneficial such work can be:

'Life story work can increase a child's sense of self-worth, because, sadly, at the back of the minds of nearly all children separated from their families of origin is the thought that they are worthless and unlovable. They blame themselves for the actions of adults. If they have been abandoned, neglected or injured by their parents or wider family they are convinced that they brought it on themselves. Life story work gives you the opportunity to show them why they should be proud of themselves, and this positive attitude should be evident in any book, video or other record which results.'
(1993, p6)

Trauma puts us in situations in which it is hard to make sense of what has happened, to retain a coherent thread of meaning. Kahr reflects this in arguing that he, 'came to the conclusion that it is not primarily the recounting of a story that is therapeutic, but the making of it and the kind of work that goes into this – for making involves grappling with chaos' (2000, p113). Of course, this is very significant for children who have been sexually abused and experienced trauma as a consequence. Rose and Philpot reinforce this point when they quote the comment of Vaughan (2003, p160) that: 'In our experience children, just as much as adults, need to develop coherent narratives and that while this can be a difficult and complex process it is an essential one' (2005, p15).

When carried out skilfully, life story work can complement well the individual therapy being conducted alongside it. It can help the child to move away from the painful confusion and thereby develop a stronger sense of self and self-worth. This, again, fits well with our emphasis on the spiritual dimension of trauma. If we understand trauma, as we noted earlier, as an assault on the self, then life story work is a key part of rebuilding that self, of helping a child create a more positive sense of their identity and how they fit into the wider world. It in this sense that life story work, as a process of meaning making, is in effect a spiritual enterprise.

Therapeutic parenting

Recovery from trauma takes time, and very many abused children will need to be cared for away from their family home (for example, where a family member was the perpetrator and remains within the household). Substitute carers, whether foster carers or residential care staff, need to be well equipped (properly trained and supported) if they are to play an important role in the child's recovery – hence a whole chapter (Chapter 8) on the need to get the staff support issues right.

Foster carers and professional staff working with traumatised children face a range of challenges, as Levy and Orlans (1998) acknowledge. They point out that abused children are likely to find it difficult to give and receive love and affection. They may constantly defy parental authority and can be physically and emotionally abusive to others. Such reactions can, of course, create immense difficulties for carers and their families. It is therefore important that how abused children are cared for is handled carefully and wisely. This is precisely what the notion of 'therapeutic parenting' is all about.

Practice focus 2.2

When the first children came to SACCS, we wanted their behaviour to be lovingly contained by the care staff whilst the therapeutic work was carried out by the child's therapist.

It soon became apparent that the stories the children arrived with were often either inadequate or at worst untrue. Sometimes they had acquired the wrong name along the way. They had lost siblings and even parents whilst in the care system. Their stories were often incomplete and frequently inaccurate. In order for the children to be able to move on in their lives it was important that they knew and understood where they had come from. We created a specialist team to research the child's past, by going through local authority files, and interviewing everyone who was important in the child's past, including parents – even or especially if they were also the abuser – extended family, other carers, teachers if appropriate, doctors, health visitors and others. The broken shards of the child's life, once gathered, were made sense of, and the child was, at their own pace, helped to integrate the truth of what had happened to them, to piece by piece put it in place, so that it could then be processed as part of the ongoing work with the child and they could be helped to get some perspective in their lives.

At about the same time, we realised that we had a very valuable resource, in so far as the care staff in the houses were concerned. The therapists were only able to see the children for an hour a week, but the care staff were with them the rest of the time. We began to develop the idea of therapeutic parenting, which implied a very different approach. We created a different model of training that eventually became a foundation degree that was mandatory for all care staff. Through supervision they developed reflective practice where they could look at what was happening for themselves and reflect how that might be mirroring what was happening in the house and in their team. They had external consultants who came in on a regular basis to support the teams and help them make sense of what was happening.

This three-pronged approach was instrumental in creating our practice and it depended on everyone communicating openly and co-operating with each other.

Pughe and Philpot describe the idea helpfully when they comment that:

'Therapeutic parenting is very much about nurture, offering a traumatised child, actually and symbolically, that care, attention and nurture which she will have been denied in growing up. Nurture perhaps too captures something of the idea of total care – physical and emotional – which the good parent offers the child.'
(2007, p11)

An important feature of this is how day-to-day caring is handled sensitively and effectively. For example, how issues relating to food are handled can be very significant. Tomlinson (2004) points out that: 'the provision of food is clearly of central importance (see Hancock *et al*, 1990) ... Food can have associations for children that are related to their experiences of trauma and abuse' (p39). The link between food, as physical nurturance, and well-being (emotional nurturance) is a long-established one. Food consumption can reflect and manifest underlying problems (emotional distress leading to anorexia or bulimia, for example), while also, when well managed, offer considerable comfort and support and reinforce a sense of security.

Therapeutic parenting provides a sound foundation of care and support on which the combination of individual therapy and life story work can build recovery. In this way the three core elements of the Walsh Recovery Programme therapeutic approach support one another. They provide a helpful interlocking framework of supportive interventions that can make a significant positive impact. Together they add up to a more holistic picture of the child's needs and circumstances.

Figure 2.1: The three elements

The 24 outcomes

In recent years we have seen an increasing emphasis on the importance of outcomes in the social welfare field – that is, of being clear about what we are trying to achieve (Thompson, 2008). In many respects the Walsh Recovery Programme (WRP) anticipated this by developing an explicit set of outcomes that guide practice and give a benchmark from which to judge the extent of progress.

The 24 outcomes are identified by Tomlinson and Philpot as follows. For each one, it can be established whether or not it can be said to be applicable to the child concerned:

- has a sense of self of whom she is and where she has been
- has an understanding of her past history and experiences
- is able to show appropriate reactions
- has developed internal controls
- is able to make use of opportunities
- is able to make appropriate choices
- is able to make appropriate adult and peer relationships
- is making academic progress
- is able to take responsibility

- has developed conscience

- is no longer hurting herself or others

- is developing insights

- has completed important developmental tasks

- has developed cause and effect thinking

- understands sequences

- has developed motor skills

- has developed abstract thinking

- has improved physical health

- has normal sleeping habits

- has normal personal hygiene

- has normal eating behaviours

- has normal body language

- has normal self-image

- is able to make positive contributions

(2008, pp39-45)

Mary and her team produced extensive documentation and provided a great deal of training to explore what is meant by each of these outcomes and how they are likely to manifest themselves in the child's day-to-day life. It is also recognised that these need to be understood in the context of cultural diversity (for example, in terms of what is considered normal or acceptable being different in different cultural settings).

What is particularly significant about these 24 outcomes is that they offer a very thorough and detailed overview of the child and their circumstances. This can help to ensure that key areas are not missed out of the picture. What this detailed approach also does is offer a basis of confidence – for the child, who can be reassured by how much effort is going into understanding them and addressing their issues, and for staff and foster carers, who can feel confident in having a thorough, structured framework to work to.

The developmental areas

Cutting across the 24 outcomes is an assessment framework structured around six areas of development. These are:

- **Learning**. Children who have been traumatised can be blocked in their learning, and so working towards freeing them up to be open to learning again is an important part of recovery. Plotting their progress in this regard is therefore an important part of the process. Poor educational outcomes can severely hold back a child in later life, and so these issues are important for that reason. However, it is not just about academic-type learning and qualifications, it is also about enabling the child to develop their learning skills so that they can learn more about life, including learning about their own needs, challenges and recovery.

- **Physical development**. Psychological trauma can also have physical consequences and can, for example, act as an impediment to growth and development. Milestones of physical growth being achieved is therefore a good sign. The stress and distress associated with trauma can undermine the functioning of the immune system and thereby leave the child more open to infection. In addition, stress and distress can result in loss of appetite, poor physical growth and thus poor development overall.

- **Emotional development**. The emotional consequences of abuse and trauma can be both extensive and profound, wreaking havoc in young lives. However, it is possible for emotional development to be helped by appropriate input, and this is a major feature of the WRP approach. There has been much talk of emotional intelligence and emotional resilience in recent years, but the major focus of such work has mainly been on adults. How children learn to manage emotions (their own and other people's) is an important topic in its own right, but the issues involved are particularly significant for children who have been abused and therefore exposed to the confusing and frightening maelstrom of feelings associated with such experiences.

- **Attachment**. The attachments young children form have long been recognised as highly significant in shaping future relationships and emotional responses. Sexual abuse is an abuse of many things – power, trust, innocence – and we need to include an abuse of attachment in this list. Consider how grooming works, for example, where an exploitative attachment is made specifically to facilitate abuse. In grooming, a perpetrator deliberately wins the trust of a child with the sole intention of using that trust as a means of gaining sexual gratification. It is often the attachment that will prevent the child from disclosing the abuse, knowing that somebody they have an important emotional bond with will 'get into trouble' if they disclose what has happened, as perpetrators who use grooming are generally aware. Indeed, it is not unusual for a perpetrator to use emotional pressure deliberately, such as 'If you tell anyone, I will go to prison' to prevent the abuse coming to light. This, of course, then adds a further layer of emotional abuse to the impact of the sexual abuse.

- **Identity**. One of the well-documented effects of trauma is an undermining of identity, resulting in difficulty in maintaining a coherent sense of self which allows us to feel comfortable 'within our own skin'. Traumatised children are likely to experience 'ontological insecurity' (Thompson & Walsh, 2010), which means that they are confused and uncertain about who they are and how they fit into the wider world. This sort of spiritual confusion is something that recovery needs to address. The three-pronged approach seeks to address this issue by reinforcing a positive sense of identity consistently across all three elements of the programme.

- **Social and communicative development**. Of course, children do not live in a vacuum, and they need to be able to relate to others, to develop communication and social interaction skills. The high level of mistrust associated with abuse can be a significant impediment to this, and so recovery efforts need to focus on this aspect of the child's development. Children will, of course, vary in their rate of development in these areas, but, with skill and experience, it is possible to assess how much progress a child is making in relation to these important aspects of development.

These six areas of development are monitored and recorded on a six-element assessment wheel, as illustrated in Figure 2.2 on p56. This enables staff involved in the WRP process to have a relatively clear picture of the progress being made (and thus the progress yet to be made). Progress along each of the three elements – individual therapy, life story and therapeutic parenting – is plotted from the centre outwards, using colour coding to distinguish each of the strands.

Figure 2.2: The assessment wheel

ASSESSMENT SCORE SUMMARY

NAME:_____ DATE:_____

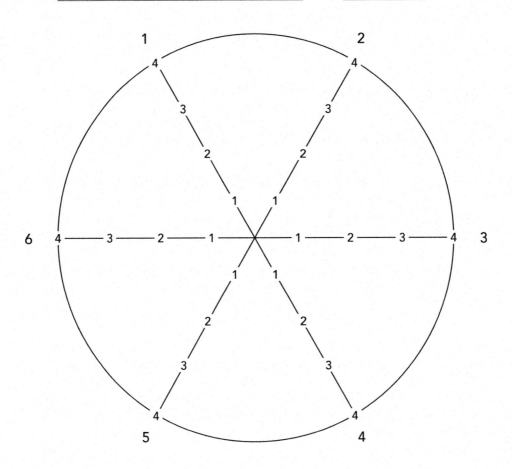

1 = Learning, 2 = Physical Development, 3 = Emotional Development,
4 = Attachment, 5 = Identity, 6 = Social & Communicative Development

KEY
KEY
Red –   Therapy
Green – Life story
Blue –   Therapeutic parenting

The value base

From an early stage it was recognised that the important work undertaken by Mary and her team needed to be underpinned by an explicit set of values. These formed the basis of the principles that should be guiding the practice of all involved in the trauma recovery enterprise.

Figure 2.3: The value base

The emphasis on values is an important part of the history of this approach, in so far as it indicates that the endeavour is rooted in a strong ethical commitment to doing right by children – especially those children who have been wronged by exploitation and abuse.

Integrating the components

For ease of exposition, we have separated out the different elements of the WRP. However, it is important to note that, in reality, it is an integrated and dynamic system; a holistic approach that brings the different elements together in meaningful ways. It is integrated in the sense that different components will influence one another. For example, physical development will have an effect on identity in terms of physical appearance and both of these can have an effect on emotional development (such as in situations where a child is being bullied because of their physical appearance). In turn, emotional issues, as mentioned above, can affect physical development, through appetite suppression for example, or, at the other extreme, through excessive 'comfort eating'. It is dynamic in the sense that it is a constantly moving and evolving picture, and so a static snapshot will not suffice. Assessment needs to be an ongoing activity, an iterative process whereby what is known, what is happening and what needs to happen are constantly being reviewed.

Key point

The Walsh Recovery Programme's three-pronged approach needs to be understood as a set of constantly evolving interactions across the three dimensions, and not as a static model with three unconnected elements.

Through the training of their own staff and training provided for a wide range of organisations, plus input to the Foundation Degree in Therapeutic Child Care developed in conjunction with a local university, great emphasis is placed on a holistic approach that integrates the three therapeutic modalities (individual therapy, life story work and therapeutic parenting), the 24 outcomes and the six developmental areas – all within a context of being child centred.

This holistic approach is reflected in the comments of Thomas and Philpot (2009), who argue that there are three factors that are key to the Walsh Recovery Programme and which act as a form of glue to help bind the elements together:

■ **Safety (in place of fear)**. As we shall see in Chapter 4, abuse and trauma are associated with horror and terror. There must therefore be a strong commitment to creating safety – both physical and emotional – for the child, so that they can take the risks needed to grow and recover. If we are not able to create a safe environment for children it is highly unlikely that they will be prepared to move forward as part of a process of recovery, to move beyond their fear.

■ **Containment (in place of disintegration)**. This takes us back to the importance of emotional holding or containment that we mentioned earlier. It is not just about *being* safe (physically), it is also about *feeling* safe (emotionally). Being contained (or 'held') is an important part of emotional security. Recovery needs to involve this too – not only leaving the fear behind, but also feeling that there are people who care enough and who are strong, reliable and trustworthy enough to protect them and provide a foundation of security.

- **Attachment (in place of detachment)**. Forming an attachment involves a significant level of trust. Child abuse, as we have already discussed, constitutes an abuse of trust. It is not surprising, therefore, that abused children are likely to find it very difficult to trust people and form new attachments. Rebuilding trust and creating new attachments, although a very difficult undertaking, are essential components of recovery.

They go on to explain that the model is based on:

- **Openness, not secrecy**. This brings us back to the themes of secrecy and denial discussed earlier. Developing openness is a fundamental part of building trust, although it has to be recognised that this can be more difficult than it sounds. The process can be begun in the short term, but it is likely to need longer-term support to make a positive difference to a child's ability and willingness to trust.

- **Communication, not avoidance**. The issues that need to be discussed can be painful, confusing, embarrassing and distressing for both the children who have had abusive experiences and the adults who are trying to help them recover. It is therefore very easy to slip into patterns of avoidance to make life seem more comfortable. This is, of course, a significant mistake, as it is vitally important that we keep the channels of communication open. This brings us back to the question of emotional intelligence, part of which is to be able not only to communicate our own feelings effectively and appropriately, but also to be able to 'read' other people's feelings and communicate appropriately. It is a matter of working *with* emotional issues, rather than letting the emotions in any given situation work *against* us.

- **Predictability, not inconsistency**. There are inevitably unpredictable elements in life (Taleb, 2010), but there is also much that is regular and predictable, and which can be a source of comfort, stability, reassurance and security. There is therefore much to be gained from avoiding inconsistencies and thereby contributing to the settling rhythms of consistency. Indeed, predictability and consistency are like the rhythm in music – they play an important role in laying the foundations.

The Mary Walsh Approach has grown and developed over the years and will no doubt continue to develop over time, as new understandings about the complexities of trauma emerge. It by no means answers all our questions about abuse-related trauma, as no approach could do that, but it does offer a helpful platform from which to develop our responses – as professionals and as a society more broadly – to the tragedies of child abuse.

Conclusion

Over its 25-year history, SACCS increased in size by 5,000 per cent (from five staff to 250) and developed a huge footprint of influence. As discussed in Chapter 1, Mary developed an organisation that 'punches above its weight' – that is, it has had a positive impact on professional practice far out of proportion for its size. A key factor in its success has been its unstinting insistence on being child centred. As Rymaszewska and Philpot (2006) put it, reflecting Mary's philosophy: 'A child who has been abused and is traumatised is first and foremost a child' (p29). They are not a 'case', not a 'commodity', not a helpless 'victim', not an object of concern, but a child, a vulnerable human being in need of care and protection.

The WRP evolved from years of practice, but this does not mean that it has no theoretical underpinnings. Indeed, there is a significant theory base informing the practice development. A review of these key ideas will be our next topic and will form the basis of Chapter 3.

Points to ponder

1. Making sure that abused children are made safe is important work, but it is not enough on its own. Why do you think that is?

2. How might life story work help a child who has been abused and traumatised?

3. Why is the notion of emotional intelligence so important?

Exercise

Why is it important to understand the three elements as interacting and evolving, rather than as separate and static? What consequences would there be for the child in recovery and the people helping if the three elements were not properly integrated? Think about this in terms of both short-term and long-term consequences.

Chapter 3: The journey of ideas

Introduction

In this chapter we explore the key ideas that have informed our practice in general and the development of the WRP in particular. The discussion is not comprehensive, of course, as an exhaustive analysis of the wide range of ideas drawn upon could easily take up a whole book in its own right. Our focus, then, is necessarily selective and thus limited to what we see as some of the core ideas.

The relationship between theory (ideas) and practice (actions) is a complex one, but it is also an important one (Thompson, 2000). It is not simply a matter of taking ideas and 'applying' them to practice in a simple, straightforward or direct way (what Schön (1983) described as a 'technical rationality' approach), as that is not what happens in the complexities of practice (the 'swampy lowlands', to use Schön's colourful phrase). Thompson (2017a) has developed a more realistic appraisal of how theory and practice interconnect by introducing the notion of 'theorising practice'. This relates to a process which begins with practice and then involves drawing on the professional knowledge base (theory, research and practice wisdom developed over time) as and when required to suit the specific circumstances. The reflective practitioner is therefore someone who is able to make sense of their practice experiences by drawing on their professional knowledge base in this way, and the critically reflective practitioner is someone who does so by engaging with the professional knowledge base *critically* – that is, not simply taking it at face value (Thompson & Thompson, 2018).

The ideas that are presented in this chapter represent a significant part of the theory base that therapeutic trauma work has drawn upon, sometimes explicitly, sometimes implicitly, to make sure that the practice has been (and continues to be) informed and critical practice. It is, then, not simply a matter of dogmatically following a set of received ideas. It is rather a matter of engaging critically with a well-established knowledge base and tailoring it creatively to suit the specific circumstances of each child and their needs.

Key point

To make sure that we are as effective as possible in helping children recover from trauma, we need to avoid the mistake of driving a wedge between theory and practice. We need to recognise that we are dealing with complex issues, and so we need a good theoretical understanding in order to make sense of the situations we are involved in.

The point was made earlier that no adequate theory of childhood trauma has yet been developed, although new thinking and neuroscience have added new dimensions, with contributions from Perry and Szalavitz (2017), Ziegler (2002) and Ogden *et al* (2006). Clearly, the trauma-informed practice that is emerging has contributed to thinking and service provision. There is still a long way to go yet before we can claim to have developed a sufficient understanding. However, what follows represents some of the key elements of what we do understand and the sharing of the journey of practice and the training of residential therapeutic parents developed by Mary and her team.

Trauma

'Trauma' comes from the Greek word for wound. In a medical context it is used to refer to physical wounds, but for some time now it has also been used in a more metaphorical sense to refer to psychological wounds. A traumatic experience is therefore one that results in lasting psychological harm. Trauma is often described as an emotional wound, but we need to be clear that the harm experienced can also affect thinking and behaviour, and also has social and spiritual (or existential) consequences (see Thompson & Walsh, 2010). Lasting psychological harm should therefore be understood to encompass cognitive, behavioural, social and spiritual aspects as well as emotional. That is, we need to understand trauma *holistically* (Thompson, 2012).

Figure 3.1: The four elements of a holistic approach

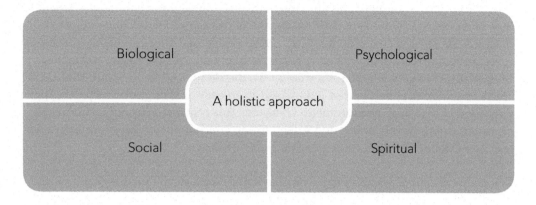

In particular, it is important to be aware that trauma is a social phenomenon as well as a psychological one (Alexander, 2012). This is because:

i. trauma tends to have a significant impact on social relationships (within the family and broader social networks)
ii. experiences of, and reactions to, trauma differ from society to society, culture to culture (Bracken, 2002).

We will discuss the significance of the social context below.

Trauma can arise from a variety of causes. These include (but are not limited to):

■ bereavement or other significant losses

■ disaster situations

■ witnessing a death

■ war and terror

■ abuse and neglect.

What we need to keep clearly in our minds is that children traumatised by abuse do not become immune to these other potential sources of trauma. It is therefore quite possible that children traumatised by abusive incidents can also be further traumatised by other experiences in their lives. Indeed, the experience of abuse can make some other types of potentially traumatic experience more likely (being removed from home, for example).

Abuse

Corby *et al* (2013) highlight the difficulties involved in defining child abuse when they point out that notions of child abuse and neglect are complex and subject to constant change and realignment. They acknowledge that they are highly contested concepts that are underpinned by various political and cultural factors specific to the particular society in which they occur. We therefore need to recognise that child abuse is not a phenomenon that lends itself to an easy or straightforward definition that allows for ease of measurement. Of course, this contrasts strongly with media representations of child abuse and safeguarding which are generally simplistic and one dimensional. We shall return to this point below.

The legal concept of 'significant harm' is a helpful one, in so far as it captures the idea that abuse harms children, although what constitutes significant harm is in itself a complex and contested notion. In line with the holistic understanding of abuse and trauma, we need to be aware that the harm can be physical, psychological, social and spiritual. Chapter 4 explores these issues in more depth.

Practice focus 3.1

Staff came to the consultancy meeting saying they felt really bad because they couldn't 'take' to a boy who was only six and living in their care. They were helped to see that this was important information and we needed to look at why they were feeling that way.

They said he was shallow and would talk to anyone on the street about his dad weeing in his mouth. We needed to look at what that meant to him. He would only have been about three-years old and almost certainly he would have had to be held down. His father's adult penis would have been put near or in his mouth and he would probably have had his nose held, so that he would open his mouth. Then noxious liquid, either urine or ejaculate, poured into his mouth. He wouldn't have been able to swallow or to breathe. He must have been very frightened and he probably thought he was going to die. The issue for him, and what he was trying to communicate to someone, anyone, was 'did I nearly die?' When the staff realised that this was what was going on, their attitude changed, and, as they responded to him more positively, so his behaviour changed.

Mary and her team concerned themselves primarily with addressing sexual abuse, although different forms of abuse (physical, emotional, neglect) often coincide. Indeed, sexual abuse is generally accompanied by a significant component of emotional abuse. It could even be argued that sexual abuse is itself substantially a form of emotional abuse, and it is this that serves as a major contributory factor in the development of a traumatic response.

Although we have discussed abuse and trauma separately, what has been key to the development of Mary's approach is the recognition of the link between them. Arguably, one of the most significant causes of trauma is child abuse. There is now a growing literature base that draws links between childhood trauma and mental health problems in later life (Bentall, 2010). Indeed, it is increasingly being recognised that early life trauma and other adverse childhood experiences (ACEs) are very significant in the development of mental health problems (Thompson, 2019a).

The personal violation involved in acts of abuse can lead to distress and disorientation of a sufficient magnitude to lead to trauma. Hosin (2007) explains that repeated events (as in the case of a child who is repeatedly abused before their plight comes to light) can have more devastating effects than a single traumatic experience. Thompson (2017d) reinforces this point when she explores how trauma can arise from a series of distressing and challenging incidents over time, rather than one single dramatic event. In view of the different types of harm associated with abuse, child abuse can be understood as not only a common cause of trauma, but also an especially harmful one.

Attachment

The concept of attachment and its associated theory base have a long history in child care. Its origins are strongly associated with the work of John Bowlby (1969; 1979). His original version of attachment theory can be criticised for its gender bias and lack of sociological awareness. For example, it referred to the role of the mother, rather than the primary caregiver, and, in so doing, failed to acknowledge that it is possible for other caregivers to be the key person(s). It thereby failed to incorporate wider sociological issues that have an influence on a child's development (see the discussion below of the social context). It can also be criticised in part for its 'biological reductionism' – that is, its tendency to overstate the role of biological factors in child development (we shall return to this point below when we consider developments in neuropsychology). The work of Howe (2005; 2011) has helped us to move forward in developing a more sophisticated understanding of attachment, but sadly this remains a topic prone to oversimplification.

The notion of attachment is based on the premise that infants form an emotional bond with their primary caregiver (usually, but not exclusively, their mother). This bond or 'attachment' provides a base of security from which the growing child can explore and engage with the wider world. Where such attachments are not formed or are distorted in some way, significant development problems can arise (particularly in relation to emotional responses and behaviour).

Howe (2005) identifies four different types of attachment:

Secure attachments

Howe describes these in the following terms:

'Children who find themselves in relationships with parents whose caregiving is sufficiently sensitive, loving, responsive, attuned, consistent, available and accepting develop secure attachments. Parents are interested in their infant's physical needs and states of mind. They are keen to understand their child, and to be understood by their child. This offers the prospect of a coordinated and cooperative relationship.'
(2005, p31)

This is seen as 'healthy' attachment. It avoids the problems associated with other forms of attachment. This is the sort of attachment that good parenting should aim for and which child care professionals should support, encourage and facilitate.

Avoidant attachments

This refers to situations in which the primary caregivers distance themselves from the child and their needs. In effect, they make it difficult for the child to form secure attachments because they feel uncomfortable themselves when the child shows attachment behaviours. The child learns to keep feelings of vulnerability (or other feelings that evoke discomfort in their parents) to themselves and not express them. They therefore learn how to avoid causing problems for their caregivers, but they do not learn how to elicit care and protection.

This type of attachment is more likely to occur when one or both parents (or other primary caregivers) has alcohol- or drug-related problems, has difficulties with depression or is, for whatever reason, 'emotionally absent'. Such attachments can lead to a build up of tension in the child that they find difficult to handle, and this can have lasting detrimental effects.

Ambivalent attachments

In this type of attachment, parents create problems by being preoccupied with their own needs (particularly their need for recognition and affirmation). Such parents thereby pay relatively little attention to the needs of their child and focus more on their own need for recognition. This can result in what is known as 'hyperactivated' attachment behaviours, which means that the child exaggerates their efforts to elicit care, protection and affection. It is as if they are trying to demand that they (and their needs) are noticed. In this respect it is the opposite of avoidant attachments which discourage attachment behaviours.

Once again, alcohol, illicit drug use and depression can be significant factors, and the detrimental effects for the child can be potentially lifelong.

Disorganised attachments

Howe (2005) describes this type of attachment as follows:

'Children who are parented by carers who are either frightening or frightened, or both, experience distress (Main and Hesse, 1990). Abusive and hostile carers hurt and frighten their children. Depressed, drunk or drugged parents can appear helpless, and this can also frighten children. Carers who are bedevilled by old unresolved losses and traumas from their own unhappy childhoods can feel confused and frightened whenever they find themselves being cast in the role of carer and protector by their child seeking safety and comfort. Their unresolved attachment traumas make it difficult for them to empathize with the needs and distress of their children.'
(2005, p37)

It is this fourth type of attachment that is of particular interest to us in relation to our approach to therapeutic care. Howe *et al* (1999) explain how significant it is when they argue that the disorganised (and therefore insecure) attachment pattern is strongly associated with children who have experienced significant losses and traumas and have failed to resolve them – including those arising from abuse or other such problematic situations (for example, having one or more parents who suffer from serious mental health problems or alcohol addiction).

Attachment is very significant in relation to trauma because attachments are likely to become disrupted as a result of a traumatic experience. Howe *et al* (1999) make a helpful comment in stating that such 'adverse relationships' can obstruct children's ability to develop a solid basis of social and emotional understanding. Children growing up in such problematic environments are likely to find the demands of interpersonal life challenging and distressing and therefore a considerable source of frustration. This in turn can become a significant source of problem behaviours and emotional responses.

One issue to be aware of is how a 'trauma bond' can look like a secure attachment, but is actually based on fear, not love (James, 2009). It occurs due to intense abusive experiences between a child and his/her abuser. It is very similar to Stockholm Syndrome and holds the child emotionally captive to their abuser.

Practitioners therefore need to be aware of the trauma bond when carrying out an assessment of attachment.

One reason why attachment is so significant is that there tends to be a generational 'knock on' effect. That is, children who have struggled with attachment issues can grow up to become parents who struggle to form helpful, secure attachments with their own children. This will not always be the case, of course, as some parents who had attachment difficulties in their own childhood can become all the more determined to make sure that their own children have positive attachment experiences.

Key point

A good understanding of attachment and the problems associated with it is essential for being well equipped to rise to the challenges of helping children recover from trauma.

Attachment, as a helpful explanatory concept, has featured strongly in the work of Mary and her team over the years, as they have recognised that it helps to cast significant light on the experiences of children who have been sexually abused and traumatised by that abuse. Attachment theory can also help to explain the cycle of abuse – that is, why a proportion of children who have been abused go on to become abusers themselves, in so far as they have developed disorganised attachments.

Internal working models

Closely associated with the concept of attachment is the idea of an 'internal working model'. This refers to a perspective on the world that we adopt from our early childhood experiences. It is a blueprint for how we interact with the world. Usually formed between 12 and 18 months, it is quite difficult to change. It shapes how we see ourselves, our parents and the world around us. For most of us, thankfully, these are positive messages: 'my parents look after me and meet my needs'; 'the world is a benign place that I can explore safely'; and 'I feel safe and loved and confident'.

Children who have had abusive experiences from a very early age have a very different blueprint, which may be something like: 'My parents are dangerous and want to hurt me'; 'the world is very unsafe and I have to protect myself';

and 'I am bad and very frightened'. The internal working model is so powerful that it governs every interaction in the child's life, and they behave as if their belief system is the truth. This often evokes the response that confirms the child's beliefs.

The link with attachment theory is that it is the type of attachment(s) we have formed that will have a strong influence on our internal working model. Prior and Glaser capture the idea well when they explain that:

'Bowlby likened internal working models to cognitive maps, a map being a "coded representation of selected aspects of whatever is mapped" (Bowlby, 1969, p80). A map, however, as Bowlby points out, is a static representation. Working models, on the other hand, enable the individual to "conduct ... small-scale experiments within the head" (p81). Working models comprise two parts, an environmental model, based on accumulated experience, and an organismic model, based on self-knowledge of one's skills and potentialities.'
(2006, p21)

An internal working model can therefore be seen as a fundamental basis for meaning making, for making sense of our world, an important topic we will discuss below, and one that brings us back to the spiritual element of our holistic model. Dallos (2006) links this to wider systems of communication. He argues that it is important to see internal working models as factors that both shape and are shaped by processes of communication. For example, the ability of children to express their needs and feelings will play a significant role in shaping how others respond to them. In turn, these responses influence, sustain and consolidate the internal working model. It is therefore a *psychosocial* process – the psychological affects the wider sociological factors (social interaction), which then affect the psychological; a dynamic or 'dialectical' relationship is established, with each element influencing the other on an ongoing basis.

This helps to locate the notions of working model and attachment in a wider social field and thereby frees it up from the common criticism that such ideas are too individualistic (or 'atomistic', to use the technical term) and not adequately rooted in the vitally important social sphere. No child lives in a social vacuum, and so it is important that we incorporate social elements into our analysis and understanding (see Chapter 7 for further discussion of these and related issues).

The internal working model concept can be linked to the idea of narratives as the basis of our social life. We make sense of our lives through creating narratives, or stories, that link together the disparate elements of our experiences and provide us with a coherent sense of who we are – what is often referred to as a 'self-narrative'. These narratives are, of course, unique to each of us, reflecting our unique circumstances and our unique responses to them, but there will also be wider social patterns that influence the development of such narratives (through the influence of culture, for example), so once again we are in *psychosocial* territory, the place where social and psychological factors meet and influence one another.

Emotional holding

In the context of working with traumatised or otherwise emotionally troubled children or young people, 'holding' refers to providing a setting and atmosphere in which children can feel safe to express their feelings, without fear of any sort of recrimination or adverse outcome; where their powerful emotions can be safely 'contained' without causing further problems and without being unduly restricted (Weld, 2009). Individual therapy, life story work and therapeutic parenting can all play an important role in promoting an environment of holding (or 'containment', as Bion called it (1962)). It is also important that staff working with traumatised children are 'held' (Kahn, 2005). We shall return to this point in Chapter 8, but for now it is worth noting that the consequences of not putting emotional holding can be severe in terms of the potential harm that can be done by being exposed to intense emotionality without adequate support.

The Mary Walsh Approach has been developed with the concept of 'holding' in mind, for both children and adults. In a sense, this is a way of forming new, secure attachments. It is a matter of those working with children, being attentive to them and giving a clear, positive message that they are safe, that it is OK for them to express their emotions and verbalise their fears, their frustrations and their pain, as well as their hopes, aspirations and desires. Holding means creating an environment where there is no sense that there are taboos around the expression of emotion, however uncomfortable that may be for the adults involved. It also involves giving the message that, while it is acceptable to vent feelings, there are boundaries and controls set by caring adults that help to create a sense of security.

This can be understood as a two-stage process: first, creating the atmosphere in which emotional expression is not only allowed, but actually encouraged and supported; and second, helping children and adults to learn which forms of emotional expression are positive, constructive and helpful and which are negative, destructive and problematic.

Neuropsychology

There has been major emphasis on developments in neuropsychology in recent years. These developments have enabled us to improve our understanding of what happens in a child's brain and nervous system when they experience trauma. As Barton *et al* explain:

'Experiences of trauma create states of hyperarousal and fear in children that cause the brain to produce adrenalin, which stimulates the mind and body to be prepared to fight or take flight. This can be seen as a normal healthy response to danger that improves the likelihood for survival. We take flight from the danger rather than stay in its proximity. However, when a child is continually in a state of danger, the brain is in a constant state of arousal and the excess of adrenalin that is produced actually damages the brain's development. Additionally, the part of the brain that reads danger signals becomes hypervigilant and begins to exaggerate warning signals. Danger is increasingly read into situations that are not actually dangerous. Hence the child becomes highly anxious and hyperaroused by ordinary everyday experiences.'
(2012, p53)

Ziegler (2002) comments that the brain continues to signal to the body that trauma is still occurring long after the actual trauma has ceased to apply (hence the analogy of a trauma as a wound that has yet to heal).

It is clear that neuropsychology has an important part to play, but again we need to be wary of biological reductionism – that is, the tendency to reduce the holistic, multidimensional picture we need in order to make sense of the complexities involved to a single-level explanation. In other words, there is indeed a biological dimension to trauma, but we have to make sure that we do not allow the current emphasis on neuropsychology to seduce us into neglecting the other key dimensions (psychological, sociological and spiritual).

The basic theoretical flaw on which such approaches are based is the confusion of biological *channelling* with biological *causality*. All human experience, with its complex psychological, social and spiritual roots, manifests itself through biological channels (hence the term 'channelling'), as no human being could exist without a biological body, but it would be a mistake to assume that our experiences are 'caused' by our biology. For example, someone who is grieving may be experiencing a range of significant bodily sensations as a result of their grief, but it would be a gross distortion to attribute their grief to biological causes. It would oversimplify a very complex set of processes and, at the same time seriously undervalue the significance of psychological, social and spiritual factors in shaping a child's experience. All human experience is biologically channelled, but this does not mean that it is necessarily biologically caused. In other words, biology is the vehicle through which we live our lives, but it is not the driver. It would be a significant mistake to ignore the biological aspects of trauma, but it would also be a mistake to overemphasise their role at the expense of other important considerations.

Key point

There have been some exciting and insightful developments in neuropsychology in recent years, but we must not allow this progress to lead us into overemphasising the biological dimension and neglecting the importance of other significant dimensions of human experience in general, and of trauma in particular.

One very positive aspect of the new understanding neuropsychology has brought is the recognition that it is possible for children to build new neural pathways, to find new ways of making sense of the world and responding to it. This is known as 'plasticity' and refers to the possibility to alter previously established patterns of behaviour and emotional response. This runs counter to the traditional Freudian notion that, by the age of five, a child's personality is irrevocably set for the most part.

This advance in our knowledge helps to affirm the key point that trauma is not a life sentence. This can be a significant source of hope and thus of motivation. However, as we shall see below, hope is a double-edged sword, as it can also be a source of difficulties.

Meaning and narrative

Life can be understood to have both subjective (internal) and objective (external) dimensions. There is, of course, a world out there, in an objective sense, but there are also the necessary subjective interpretations that enable us to make sense of our experience (hence the fact that two different people can be present in the same situation but interpret it in very different ways). As human beings, we are in effect 'meaning-making creatures' – that is, we have to make sense of our experiences; we cannot simply take them at face value as 'objective' reality.

Meaning therefore acts as a form of linking thread that enables us to make sense of our life. However, the meanings we draw to make sense of what we encounter do not exist in isolation. They become part of a broader tapestry, a meaningful picture of interrelationships. As we mentioned earlier, the technical term for this is a 'narrative', a story that connects different elements of our experience together in a meaningful way. This takes us back to our discussion of life story work, which can be understood as a form of 'narrative therapy' (Dallos, 2006), helping children to develop a positive, empowering narrative that can help them dispel the confusion and pain associated with abuse.

Key point

Stories, or 'narratives', are the building blocks through which we develop meaningful understandings of our lives and circumstances. Children who have been abused are likely to have developed unhelpful, disempowering narratives. A key part of recovery is helping children to develop more positive, empowering narratives.

When it comes to trying to understand trauma – which can have such a devastating effect on our sense of who we are, how we fit into the world and how we find security within it – meaning is especially significant. Recovering from trauma can be understood as being, to a large extent, a process of what Neimeyer (2001; 2010) calls 'meaning reconstruction'. Neimeyer and Anderson explain:

'Only the most peripheral of losses leave us substantially unchanged; the losses of central people, places and projects that anchor our sense of self force a (sometimes radical) reordering of the stories of our lives, triggering the 're-authorship' of a new life narrative that integrates the loss into the plot structure of our biography (Neimeyer and Levitt, 2001).'
(2002, pp50–51)

The basic idea behind meaning reconstruction theory is that, when we lose someone or something important to us, we also lose what they meant to us, in the sense that we have to reconfigure the part they played in our life. For example, if we lose someone we regarded as a mentor, then we need to think anew about where that leaves us, where else we might get guidance from – in other words, how we fill the gap left by that person. In this way we can understand grieving as the process of constructing new meanings or rewriting our narrative (hence the term, meaning reconstruction theory).

For young children, whose grasp of their own sense of biography is still relatively undeveloped, this can be particularly significant, hence the emphasis on life story work in the WRP (Rose & Philpot, 2005). Given our earlier point that being abused involves a range of significant losses, the role of meaning reconstruction through life story work can be seen to be a potentially very productive one, especially when supplemented by individual therapy and therapeutic parenting.

Another important aspect of meaning making is what Fahlberg (1994) called 'magical thinking'. Thomas and Philpot explain:

'Magical thinking is a way children fill in the gaps in their knowledge. When they don't know, they make it up. For example, a foster placement breaks down and the child is moved to a new home but why did the breakdown happen? If the child blames herself for the breakdown (as she may well do), then she will conclude the same again when the next breakdown occurs (as well it might). It is safer for the child to believe this but it only adds to her confusion about why she is where she is.' (2009, p43)

This reflects how narratives work. When our 'story' is disrupted we feel the need to make it whole again, as Thomas and Philpot put it, to fill in the gaps. In a situation characterised by fear and emotional pain, there is a likelihood that the gaps will be filled with worry, anxiety and even terror. The result can be that confidence and self-esteem become difficult to maintain, even to the point where self-loathing emerges, reflecting the shame, embarrassment and stigma associated with abuse. In such circumstances, it is not surprising that children who have been abused feel 'dirty' and 'unworthy'. This, combined with the sense of guilt commonly associated with grieving (even when there is actually nothing to feel guilty about – Thompson, 2012), will often lead children to assume that the abuse is their fault. The 'magical thinking' fills in the gaps in their narrative by enabling them to make sense (mistakenly, of course) of the abuse as something they have done wrong. As well as the emotional harm this does, in many cases it will also, unfortunately, serve as an obstacle to disclosure of the abuse.

Both life story work and individual therapy can help a child to let go of problematic, disempowering thoughts and replace them with more helpful, empowering ones – to develop a new narrative. However, this needs to be done skilfully and gently, as it can be dangerous to take away a child's understanding (which is serving a purpose for them) without replacing it with something else that will provide meaning and the sense of security that comes with it. This work therefore has to be done carefully, skilfully and at the child's pace.

Spirituality

Meaning is an important part of spirituality. So too are a sense of purpose and direction, our identity (our sense of who we are and how we fit into the world), connectedness (being connected to other people and thus being part of something bigger than ourselves), and a sense of awe and wonder (Thompson, 2017a). All of these can be disrupted, if not devastated, by trauma:

- **Meaning**. Trauma, and the grief reaction it provokes can seriously disrupt what Attig (2011) calls our 'assumptive world'. A traumatised child can feel that their world has been turned upside down, and so their sense of security (ontological security, to use the technical term) can be lost.

- **Purpose and direction**. With the loss of a sense of security can come the loss of purpose and direction. While younger children in particular may have little sense of where their lives are going, as they have yet to develop such ideas, trauma can nonetheless seriously disrupt their sense of what they want from their life, leaving them feeling very disoriented.

- **Identity**. Major losses, especially traumatic ones, can bring considerable confusion, and people so affected can easily find themselves saying things like: 'I don't know who I am any more'. Trauma can devastate the parameters by which we normally get a sense of who we are and how we fit into the wider scheme of things. With children there is the added factor of magical thinking, whereby they can easily assume, as we noted earlier, that the pain and suffering they are experiencing are as a result of their own unworthiness or misbehaviour, which can then further add to the confusion and distress.

- **Connectedness**. Feeling part of society and enterprises bigger than ourselves is what connectedness is all about. However, this requires a degree of trust and a willingness to commit to (potentially risky) relationships with others. Trauma can reduce that trust to a level where abused children will be very reluctant to trust others for fear of further abuse, exploitation and manipulation. This means that they are likely to opt out of activities, associations and opportunities to be part of a scheme or project, with the result that their development is adversely affected by fewer opportunities for learning, personal growth and relationship building.

- **Awe and wonder**. Children often have a very profound sense of awe and wonder that can enrich their lives significantly. However, it is very difficult to sustain such a sense when your life is characterised by fear and distress. The loss of a sense of awe and wonder can therefore be yet another loss associated with abuse and trauma. This too will then have an adverse effect on development in terms of fewer opportunities to benefit from engagement with interesting and stimulating people and places.

It should be clear, then, that the concept of spirituality is one that is very significant when it comes to understanding the impact of trauma on abused children. For this reason it has featured substantially in Mary's journey and the work of her team in establishing the WRP.

Key point

For many people, the main way they meet their spiritual needs is through religion. However, we should be careful not to make the mistake of assuming that religion is the only way of expressing spirituality or that non-religious people are somehow lacking in spirituality. The relationship between religion and spirituality is a complex one, but we must be wary of assuming that religion and spirituality are the same thing.

One further aspect of spirituality is hope, and it is to this that we now turn, as hope has particular significance in relation to abuse and trauma.

Hope

Hope is an important word in the therapeutic world's vocabulary. There is a strong commitment to creating and developing hope. Hope is a social phenomenon, in the sense that it can be increased or decreased through our interactions with other people and with wider society. Drawing on the work of Weingarten (2000, p402), Flaskas makes the important point that, 'hope is something we do with others' (2007, p28). For children, this means that the actions of the adults around them will be very significant in relation to developing or quashing hope. Trowell, in describing therapeutic work with sexually abused children, concludes that, 'The importance of sustaining hope in the child, the family and the therapist should not be underestimated' (2004, p106). Holloway and Moss (2010) also present an important discussion of hope as a feature of spirituality when they write of their 'fellow traveller' model, which refers to the value and importance of people facing distressing circumstances having the support of someone who understands and is empathic – an important consideration when it comes to trauma recovery.

However, it is also important to recognise that hope is a double-edged sword, in the sense that it can have a very positive effect in helping children move forward on the one hand, but can also cause problems on the other. We are referring to situations where too strong a reliance on hope can distort a situation. A classic example of this is the 'rule of optimism' (Dingwall *et al*, 1983), which describes the pitfall of child protection workers attributing too much significance to improvements in a situation where there are risks of abuse to a child and/or adopting too favourable a view of the parents' approach to their children. A degree of improvement in a situation (for example, a higher level of parental co-operation with professionals or an improvement in parenting practices) can lead to professionals being overly optimistic about the risk of harm. So, a reasonable amount of hope provides vision, it gives us helpful insights into how we can make progress and the motivation to do so. However, an unrealistic amount of hope blinds us; it distorts our perception of the situation.

What is needed, therefore, is a *balance* of hope which avoids the unhelpful extremes of hopelessness and defeatism on the one hand, and a naively unrealistic surfeit of hope on the other. This can be described as *realism* – avoiding the problems associated with an over-optimistic approach, without being equally pessimistic and leaving little or no room for hope.

Figure 3.2: The balance of hope

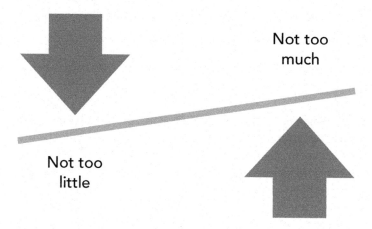

Not too
much

Not too
little

The social context

While children will, of course, have certain things in common, the therapeutic team have not allowed this sense of shared humanity to blind them to the immense diversity of the children who are abused and traumatised. There will be significant differences among children relating to race and ethnicity that can be significant in determining how best to respond (so that cultural and spiritual needs, for example, are not ignored or disrespected). Rose and Philpot point out that:

'There is plenty of evidence to a show that the denial of a child's ethnic heritage can have a deleterious effect upon mental health and that ignorance of it can, at the very least, be confusing to the child. So, helping the child connect to her religious, cultural and ethnic background is something which will also help to increase the sense of self, who she is.'
(2005, p28)

There will also be significant differences relating to gender and the complex ways in which gender differences are socially constructed (that is, shaped and defined by social processes, structures and institutions (Thompson, 2018b)). It is therefore important not to rely on the harmful, distorting gender stereotypes that abound in our society if we are not sufficiently aware of how gender features as a significant part of a child's identity and how they relate to other people. There will also, of course, be significant and potentially highly relevant differences in relation to disability, language, sexuality and other such social divisions (Thompson, 2018c). The Mary Walsh Approach has recognised the importance of tuning in to these subtle but vitally important aspects of the situations we encounter, to avoid reinforcing patterns of discrimination and oppression and thus adding to the child's difficulties at a time when they are in need of considerable help, support and protection.

These matters are sufficiently important to warrant a chapter of their own, and so we will be discussing these and related issues more fully in Chapter 7.

While there are various psychological and sociological themes that can be of value in trying to develop our understanding of childhood trauma, we should be careful not to lose sight of the fact that every child is unique and that every situation child care professionals deal with is unique. This is a key principle that resonates with the commitment to hearing the voice of each child and their distinctive story, and not simply relegating him or her to being just another example of a social pattern we can identify across a group of children.

Empowerment

The term 'empowerment' is widely used across the helping professions, but it is also one that is often misunderstood and oversimplified. As Thompson (2007) points out, there are various different types and levels of power, and so there will be different types and levels of empowerment. It is not simply a matter of giving power to people in any direct or literal sense. However, what is central to the idea of empowerment is the notion of helping people to gain greater control over their lives.

With children, this involves helping them to develop self-mastery. This is an important developmental concept which is concerned with how well a child is able to learn how to control themselves and key aspects of their environment. It is a key part of identity development. Children who have been abused can lose their sense of who they are to a certain extent (a common consequence of trauma, known as 'biographical disruption'), and their sense of self-mastery can be undermined. As Rymaszewska and Philpot put it, traumatised children 'have lost their anchor in life and with it their sense of orientation and their ability to navigate the world confidently' (2006, p36).

Empowerment can be seen as a key factor in helping children (and the adults they develop into) to move from victim to survivor and beyond. This is a fundamental part of the notion of recovery. Having the label 'victim' attached can be very disempowering. It gives a message of passivity and resignation. The notion of survivor, by contrast, implies a person who has been abused but who is able to recognise that they can move on from this: 'Somebody did something terrible to me, but that was then and this is now'.

Key point

The point is often made that child abuse involves the abuse of power. This is certainly true, although it happens in complex and subtle ways (see Chapter 7). However, power often works 'beneath the surface' and its role can be missed. It is therefore important that we do not lose sight of the role of power and its impact.

Recovery

Of course, it would be remiss of us to discuss the key ideas underpinning the Mary Walsh Approach to helping abused children recover from trauma not to include discussion of the very concept of recovery.

Tomlinson points out that: 'Trauma is an experience that potentially can be recovered from and even made use of' (2004, p16). The idea that trauma 'can be made use of' reflects the notion of post-traumatic growth (Tedeschi *et al*, 1998), which is based on the recognition that, however painful, harmful, destructive and devastating trauma can be, there is also the potential for there to be some type of silver lining in the form of personal growth and development. This is closely linked to the idea of 'transformational grief' (Schneider, 2012), which presents loss as not only painful and disorientating, but also as an opportunity for seeing our lives differently. Losses can, ironically, involve gains.

There is also a strong parallel here with crisis theory, which recognises that crisis intervention should be based not on helping people 'get back to normal' (crisis survival), but rather on capitalising on the energy generated by the crisis (Thompson, 2011). Crises involve our normal coping methods being overwhelmed, and our being put in a position where we need to find alternative ways of dealing with the situation. This can be very distressing, but it can also lead to personal growth in the sense that we can be forced to develop new coping methods, to move beyond our comfort zone. For example, if we normally cope with emotional pressures through physical exercise, but at a particular time cannot do so (due to illness or injury, for example), then we will find ourselves in a position where we have to find a different way of coping.

What these ideas have in common is the recognition that just 'getting over' a trauma, loss or crisis is not enough. It is not simply a matter of putting negative experiences behind us, as if we can simply disconnect ourselves from our past. Instead, what we need to do is to help people to understand what has happened to them; put it into perspective; recognise that they can go beyond what has happened to them (that was then, this is now) – that they are not trapped by it (victims); help them rebuild their lives in more positive, empowering and life-affirming ways (Rose, 2012).

This situation can be likened, as we noted earlier, to the healing involved in recovering from a physical injury, in the sense that, in both cases, wounds that are not given proper attention will not heal properly. A broken leg not properly set can lead to a permanent limp, and 'broken' thoughts and feelings can and will distort in exactly the same way. They will lead that person to do things in their adulthood that they would not otherwise have done. Consequently, the long-term effects for society can be seen as immense.

The aim at the very least is to help traumatised children avoid ongoing problems as a result of their abusive experiences and, where possible, to grow and flourish. These vitally important issues will be discussed in more detail in Chapter 5.

Conclusion

We began this chapter by commenting on the significance of the relationship between theory and practice. The therapeutic team have never pursued theoretical ideas for their own sake, but they recognise the importance of making sure that the work undertaken is rooted in *informed* practice, and not just habit, guesswork or copying others. The remainder of the chapter consisted of an overview of some of the key ideas that have helped to inform the practice of everyone involved in the enterprise (and of the organisations that have been influenced by the Mary Walsh Approach, whether through training, publications or conference presentations over the years). Of course, there is much more that could be said about each of these ideas and how they have played their part, but we have had to limit ourselves here to showing how the journey of ideas has been part of the development of this distinctive approach.

The conclusion of this chapter also brings to a close our review of how past developments have led to the current situation. In the remaining chapters we will now examine the current picture in more depth and detail, building on the foundations of understanding we hope we have managed to put in place in these first three chapters.

Chapter 4: The terror of abuse

Introduction

This chapter explores the horror of abuse and the dreadful reality of experiencing child abuse, especially sexual abuse. This involves examining what is meant by 'horror' in this context, and exploring why such matters are important in considering trauma and abuse. What will also be important in this chapter is the provision of an overview of the detrimental impact of abuse and trauma on children and the various ways in which it can ruin young lives if recovery is not facilitated.

Horror can be understood as an extreme form of fear, although, in one form at least, it is relatively common. This is in the sense of what Carroll (1990) calls 'art-horror'. He is referring in particular to the use of horror in cinema. Horror movies are a popular genre of film and a type of entertainment that has been popular across the world. Art-horror refers to the idea of having exposure to incidents that evoke horror in small doses so that, in a way, we experience some sense of excitement associated with them, but without the full impact of a genuinely horrific experience. It is similar to the idea of 'safe danger' that is a major feature of theme parks and fairground rides of various descriptions – the idea that people can experience a sense of horror without being exposed to any real, significant danger. Of course, this is very different from the reality of the horror of abuse.

One connection, however, between art-horror and the reality of abuse is the tendency to 'monsterise' perpetrators of abuse, to see them as bizarre, perhaps less than human figures who get involved in disgraceful acts towards innocent children. However, the reality is more complex, in the sense that, while perpetrators of abuse undoubtedly do horrific and monstrous things, to characterise them as 'monsters' can be very misleading, as it assumes that it will be possible to distinguish between perpetrators and ordinary people simply by looking for certain characteristics, perhaps their physical appearance, mannerisms or whatever. In reality, there is generally no specific way in which we can distinguish easily between perpetrators and non-perpetrators. The stereotype of the man in the park with a dirty mac is totally misleading and unhelpful.

For example, we could potentially show you 20 photographs of people, ten of whom were abusers and ten not, and you would have no way of knowing which is which. Child abusers generally look just like everybody else.

The concept of the abuser as a 'monster' is therefore dangerous, as it means that indicators of abuse may be missed because the absence of anything to suggest the perpetrator is a monster may disguise any potential tell-tale signs that they are engaging in abuse (for example, through grooming).

It is the behaviour of abusers that is the only way of highlighting them as perpetrators and, unfortunately, most perpetrators are sufficiently skilled to hide their abusive behaviour up to a point. What underpins such behaviour is very often an issue around arousal. All human beings experience a degree of arousal at times, including sexual arousal. Perpetrators of abuse are often characterised by an assumption that their needs in relation to arousal must be satisfied; that, once they become aroused, they must find an outlet for their desires in some way, even if the outlet is inappropriate, in terms of it being a child. This false belief that arousal needs must be satisfied, that there is no other way of dealing with them, is a major stumbling block to the protection of children from abuse.

The 'monsterising' of abusers also reflects the theme mentioned in earlier chapters of secrecy and denial as it allows people who are engaged in abusive behaviours some degree of camouflage if the majority of people are working on the false premise that they would know an abuser if they saw one. This is clearly dangerous, and so we need to be very well tuned in to the danger of monsterising and thus failing to do justice to some very complex issues.

In view of this, it is very important that we do not adopt an oversimplified view of the perpetrators of abuse. They come in all shapes and sizes, and are generally no different from other people, except for their abusive behaviour and the psychosocial issues that underpin that behaviour.

Key point

While abusers may well do monstrous things, the idea that they are 'monsters' and somehow different from everybody else gives perpetrators the opportunity to go unnoticed, for the most part behaving just like everybody else. It is not a matter of working out who looks like a monster and who does not. Rather, it is a matter of being vigilant about who may be forming inappropriate exploitative relationships with children.

In this chapter we will explore some of the key issues around the significance of living with fear, the impact of abuse in its various dimensions, in particular what we shall be calling the 'whole-life effects' of abuse, and, last but not least, we shall explore the significance of loss.

Living with fear

Carroll defines horror in the following terms:

'The word 'horror' derives from the Latin 'horrere' – to stand on end (as hair standing on end) or to bristle – and the Old French 'orror' – to bristle or to shudder. And though it need not be the case that our hair must literally stand on end … it is important to stress that the original conception of the word connected it with abnormal (from the subject's point of view) physiological state of felt agitation.' (1990, p24)

This is a helpful definition that helps us realise that horror can have an immediate physiological effect on us. However, we also have to recognise that the effect is more than physiological, in the sense that it can also have significant impact at psychological, social and spiritual levels.

This definition also implies that horror relates to specific incidents. There is a 'moment' of horror, which then subsides and our bodily reaction also subsides, quickly returning to normal. However, for abused children, such horrific moments can be very common. If they have developed a traumatic reaction to their abuse, then the sad reality is that moments of horror can become relatively 'normal' parts of their everyday life. The sense of horror becomes constant, rather than momentary. It is in this context that horror can become terror.

In everyday language, horror and terror are often used interchangeably, as if they are both synonyms for extreme fear. There is, however, a subtle but significant difference, in so far as terror implies an ongoing fear. It is in this sense that we use the term 'terrorism', the idea that terrorists are people who create not only moments of horror (for example when a bomb is exploded) but go beyond this to create an atmosphere of fear (Jackson *et al*, 2011). In effect, this is what terrorists are aiming for: not a temporary major impact, but to contribute to an ongoing atmosphere of fear which they envisage will help them to promote their cause and to achieve their aims. Terror, whether through terrorism or other means, creates a form of fear that destabilises and undermines. This is a very relevant concept, in so far as the terror of abuse (that is, the ongoing fear in addition to specific moments of horror) can be extremely detrimental for a child's well-being.

Figure 4.1: Horror vs terror

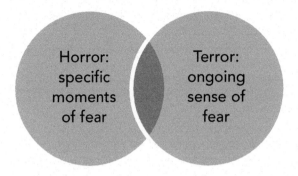

Thompson and Walsh (2010) write of the abyss that is associated with extreme fear. They relate this to the idea of existential challenges. All of us in life face certain challenges that are part and parcel of our existence (hence the term 'existential'). One particular existential challenge is facing up to our own mortality, recognising that death is an inevitable feature of life. In some ways, the trauma of abuse can be associated with our mortality, in so far as abuse can be seen as a form of death experience. Children who have been traumatised by abuse can have a sense of helplessness that can be linked to the fear of death and thus our vulnerability. This is an important aspect of abuse, the recognition that it is not a series of incidents, but, rather, has an overarching major impact on the child in terms of creating ongoing fear.

The idea of fear is commonly associated with what is known as the fight/flight response, how we respond to the increased level of adrenaline in our bloodstream which is our physiological reaction to an experience of threat. We prepare to defend ourselves (fight) or to remove ourselves from the situation (flight). However, what is often neglected is the fact that there is a third element of reaction to threat. We are referring to the notion of paralysis. A common reaction to fear is for us to freeze, so it is not simply a matter of 'fight or flight', but, rather, of 'fight, flight or freeze'.

We can become emotionally paralysed by exposure to a significant threat, feeling unable to respond. In nature, this can be a useful response – for example, when certain animals can survive a predatory attack by pretending to be dead. However, in everyday life this is of little survival value to us. Unfortunately, it is a common feature of the lives of abused children. The constant presence of fear in their lives can lead to their becoming very withdrawn, being unwilling to engage in everyday activities. This can also mean that they do not resist the abuse. It is as if they become helpless to respond in a defensive way to the threat they face. Sadly, many abusers confuse this emotional paralysis with a form of consent. It perhaps suits their purposes to see it in this way.

The idea of an ongoing sense of fear and threat can be closely linked to the important concept of 'ontological security'. Security is, of course, an everyday term, but ontological security refers to that particular type of security which is about the nature of our lives in a sense. Ontology is the study of being, and so ontological security does not mean just security in relation to a specific threat but our overall sense of security, our feeling of being safe in the world (it is therefore in some ways a spiritual concept, a point to which we will return below). Ontological security is what gives us a recognition that, while there are indeed risks in our world that we have to be wary of, overall we can feel that we are in a safe place, literally and metaphorically. What happens for a high proportion of children who are abused, however, is that ontological security is lost; their lives become, in effect, characterised by ontological insecurity, difficulty in feeling that they can be safe at all. This can be a significant aspect of trauma.

Ontological insecurity can be associated with what may be called collective traumas. Historically, the Holocaust is a powerful and tragic example of this (Bauman, 1991). More recently, Alexander (2012) has written about the ways in which societies can define certain experiences as traumatic and create a collective response to such matters. These, then, would be examples of where not only individuals, but also whole communities, experience ontological insecurity.

Horror is also an important issue to consider specifically in relation to what can so easily happen to abused children. We are referring in particular to the notion of serial placements. If the impact of trauma on abused children is not recognised (as has sadly been the case so often in the past), then the result can be that a child's placement (with foster carers or in residential care) quickly breaks down because the child is, in effect, traumatising the carers through his or her behaviour – for example, young children displaying highly sexualised behaviour. What can so easily happen is that the placement breakdown leads to the necessity of a further placement, which can also break down fairly quickly. The net result of this can be a phenomenon known as 'serial placements'. It is clear that this in itself can be understood as a form of abuse, to expose a child to the losses and other emotional demands involved in moving from placement to placement in rapid succession, with a strong likelihood that feelings of rejection and abandonment can be feeding low self-esteem and even a sense of self-loathing. The notion of serial placement is therefore an important one that we should not neglect, as it can reinforce the sense of constantly living in fear, the absence of ontological security.

Also, in terms of fear, Kahr (2002) points out that trauma can lead to a fear of psychological disintegration and thus to a 'splitting off' in the mind of traumatic experiences to prevent such a breakdown. It is as if our mind is pushing the experience away to protect ourselves from it:

'... the fear of breakdown ... the thing feared has already happened. But if early trauma has been beyond the capacity of the immature mind to survive without the risk of going to pieces or disintegrating, then the trauma may be split off in the mind as if had not yet happened, or to be more specific, as if the ego had not been in the experience. The mind then dreads ever joining up with the experience from which it has remained defensively absent – the dread being that the postponed disintegration might still happen.' (pxxiii)

Although it serves a protective function, up to a point, such a 'splitting off' is problematic because it prevents the integration of the experience and thus the emergence of new meanings. In this way, trauma can in itself create barriers to recovery, thereby sustaining over time the pain and suffering involved. We shall return to the topic of recovery in Chapter 5.

Ferguson (2004) links the idea of fear to a wider understanding of abuse as a social phenomenon. In a historical review of child abuse and child protection he shows that there has developed, through the media and the perception of the general public, a sense of fear and disgust associated with abuse. This can then come to be associated with abused children, and so what can easily happen is that the sense of horror stands in the way of professionals relating to children who have been abused:

'The underlying process here concerns how, because of their marginality, abused and neglected children raise fear and disgust. This ... has a long history. There is an underlying generative structure to practice, a structure of feeling and meanings which the historical and sociological evidence ... will show meant that not only parents but abused children have been constructed as an excluded, dangerous 'Other', a contaminating presence which required exclusion. It is here that we find the cultural roots of contemporary problems professionals have in getting close to children.'
(2004, p8)

Living with fear is therefore quite clearly a significant negative consequence of abuse. However, it is not the only one, and so it is to the wider impact of abuse that we must now turn.

The impact of abuse

The discussion here is not a comprehensive one – sadly, the various ways in which abuse can have deleterious effect on children is very broad indeed. Corby *et al* (2013) provide a fuller discussion, and it is worth consulting their work to get a sense of the broader picture. For present purposes, however, we will limit ourselves to focusing on a number of key issues.

The first of these is trauma itself. Unfortunately, in many aspects of professional practice, there has been a relatively low level of appreciation of the links between abuse and trauma. Much practice over the years has been characterised by a failure to recognise the ways in which sexual abuse in particular can result in a traumatic response on the part of the child concerned. Trauma, as we have noted, amounts to a psychosocial or existential injury. It is the way in which we encounter some horrific experience which has the effect of overwhelming our ability to cope with demands. Indeed, it goes beyond overwhelming, to devastating. As Thompson (2012) puts it, grief challenges our coping abilities, crisis overwhelms them and trauma devastates them. This in itself, of course, is sufficient to make us recognise that we need to take abuse and trauma very seriously, and so Chapter 5 will focus in particular on what is involved in promoting recovery from such trauma.

Clearly, then, trauma can be devastating in its effects. The harm it can cause can be both *intensive* (that is, very profound and detrimental) and *extensive* (that is, far reaching in its scope and consequences).

We noted earlier that trauma is a psychosocial phenomenon. It therefore has to be understood holistically, which means considering the following dimensions:

- **Cognitive**. Our thought processes and memory can both be distorted as a result of trauma. Memory is particularly significant, insofar as people who have experienced trauma often suffer from intrusive memories, or 'flashbacks'.

- **Affective**. Emotional responses to trauma are also very significant, which is not surprising given the distressing nature of trauma. The great sense of insecurity generated by trauma can lead to a lack of trust, which in turn can have significant emotional consequences.

- **Behavioural**. Withdrawal and other signs of stress are not uncommon. Also of significance are: (i) challenging behaviour – aggressive, disruptive, criminal or otherwise socially unacceptable behaviour; (ii) behaviour that may invite further abuse (sexualised behaviour, for example); and (iii) behaviour which is in itself abusive towards others.

- **Social**. This can apply to interpersonal relationships, which can suffer greatly as a result of abuse (this is partly linked to issues of trust, but see also the discussion of attachment on p65). It can also apply to social reactions to trauma in terms of such important factors as: (i) cultural patterns that shape how people respond and how they are treated when they are distressed (as Bracken puts it: 'traumatic experiences will effect different responses in individuals, depending on the culture in which they live', 2002, p73); and (ii) socio-political factors – the differential distribution of power, economic, cultural and social resources.

- **Spiritual**. Trauma is, in large measure, an assault on a person's framework of meaning and, as we shall see in Chapter 5, a focal point of therapeutic attempts to help children recover from trauma is the re-establishment of meaning or of new, more positive, life-affirming meanings.

Something that is also closely associated with trauma, which can apply in both directions (that is, it can be a cause of trauma or a result of trauma), is what Winnicott (1949) referred to as 'impingement'. Impingement involves the experience of excessive stimulation (Tomlinson, 2004). Children who are abused are faced with considerable pressures and emotional demands. There can be all sorts of internal conflicts, for example where a child is being abused, and therefore harmed, by a parent who would normally be expected to be their main protector. This can lead to a high level of emotional stimulation which can be too much for the child to process, leading to a further aspect of trauma.

Impingement is closely linked to the idea of 'engulfment', which refers to the process whereby a child feels all at sea as a result of their experience. They feel overwhelmed and uncertain in what they understandably see as very dangerous circumstances. This links closely, of course, with the idea of ontological insecurity already discussed.

Trauma in general, and impingement and engulfment in particular, can have a profoundly disruptive effect on identity, on our sense of self. Indeed, Harvey (2002) refers to trauma as 'an assault on the self'. Our sense of who we are and what our life means to us can be significantly disrupted by such experiences. In effect, our world can be turned upside down, leaving us unsure of who we are, having little sense of stability.

This can be particularly significant in terms of self-esteem, which refers to the worth or value we attribute to ourselves. If we see ourselves as unworthy, as in some way less than other people, then we will have the problem of low self-esteem (Thompson & Wallace, 2012). Low self-esteem can affect levels of confidence and our ability to lead our lives effectively (what is often referred to as self-efficacy). Trauma, then, can be understood as having a significant impact on our identity and therefore on our fundamental sense of what our life is all about. This can lead to a sense of spiritual emptiness, a disillusionment with life which can have profound, detrimental consequences in terms of an overall attitude of negativity.

This negativity can manifest itself as anomie or alienation. Anomie is a sociological term introduced by Durkheim (2006), which refers to a sense of 'normlessness'. It relates to situations where we have no sense of normality, where we feel that we are adrift in some way, and therefore feel very uncomfortable. We are likely to feel that we do not fit in, that we are not welcome in such situations, and this again can be a key factor in terms of the presence or absence of ontological security. Alienation is a similar concept in some ways, but it relates to circumstances in which we are made to feel 'other' – that is, to feel different or separated from other people, from safety and from a sense of belonging. Often the sense of stigma and shame that children feel when they have experienced abuse can contribute in major ways to both anomie and alienation. The feeling of being unclean, that is so strongly associated with sexual abuse in particular, can also be a key factor in this regard.

A further significant impact of abuse is what has come to be known as 'parentified children'. This term refers to children who, for a variety of reasons, have experienced a role reversal where they have been called upon to care for a parent. They become the parent, in effect, and their parent becomes the child (Earley & Cushway, 2002). This can happen in various ways, for example where a parent is severely disabled and requires a child to be a primary carer. This is often referred to as a practical or instrumental form of parentification. However, there can also be an emotional form of parentification (and indeed the two often go together). Emotional parentification refers to a situation where a parent has unmet emotional needs and starts to rely on their child to meet those needs. This can be a form of emotional abuse in its own right. As Hooper comments:

'*Minuchin* et al *asserted that children can experience parentification in duties such as preparing meals, doing household chores, and handling financial matters (i.e.* **instrumental parentification***) or in duties such as responding to emotional needs of the parent or siblings (including issues such as low self-esteem) or acting as the peacemaker for the family (**emotional parentification***).'*
(2007, p324)

However, there is a third form of parentification, in a sense, when sexual abuse occurs where a father, for example, uses a child as a sexual object in place of, or in addition to, his adult partner. The child feeling that they have a parental role to fulfil when they are not ready for that, and when it is not appropriate that they should have such a role anyway, can therefore be seen as a form of abuse in its own right and also a consequence of abusive behaviour on the part of one or both parents.

All in all, then, it can be seen that there are some highly significant ways in which abuse can have a very detrimental effect on children and can ruin their lives. These, it is worth emphasising again, are just some of the ways in which abuse can have a negative impact on children. However, the picture we have painted here should be sufficient to make the point that abuse is an extremely harmful phenomenon in terms of the negative effects it has on the lives of children.

Whole-life effects

We have already seen that abuse can cause many problems for children, but what also has to be recognised is that these effects can be lifelong. This can apply in a number of ways. Here we are going to focus on two in particular: first, the idea that children who have been abused can themselves go on to become abusers; and, second, the significance of abuse in childhood for later adult mental health.

It is sadly the case that a proportion of children who have been abused subsequently become abusers themselves. For some of them this will happen while they are still children. It may be that this is as a result of, for example, their own sexualised behaviour as a result of experiencing abuse. A particularly problematic time is adolescence, where a child who has had premature sexual experiences then encounters puberty and the social expectations relating to sexuality begin to be part of their lives. However, this sad phenomenon is not restricted to childhood; there will also be a proportion of children who grow up to become abusers in their adult lives. There are various potential reasons for this, and a number of theoretical approaches have been developed to try and explain what is involved in this cyclical effect of abuse whereby children who have been abused grow up to be part of the next generation of abusers (Bentovim, 2002).

Practice focus 4.1

Darren was only four when he came into care. His earliest memories were walking along pavements in the rain, being prostituted by his father. Men would be driving slowly against the kerb. He also remembers being taken onto the top of a building site where he was handed over to a strange man and his father taking money from him. He was a very disturbed young man when he came to live with us, aged seven. He had fantasies about stabbing pregnant women in general and his pregnant teacher in particular. He had had penetrative sex with other children. He was caught grooming other children in our care.

Darren engaged in therapy with enthusiasm and enjoyed learning about his arousal cycle and how he could control it. We had setbacks along the way, but Darren grew into an engaging young man who could take his place in society.

We are also now seeing growing evidence of the impact of child abuse and trauma on adult mental health. Now that the significance of child abuse is more widely known to the general public and features more in the media, including literature, drama, cinema and so on, this wider awareness has created a situation in which people who are experiencing mental health problems in adulthood have been more able to talk about their childhood experiences. The result has been a much greater tendency to believe claims of childhood abuse by adults with mental health problems, rather than dismiss them as symptoms of a mental disorder (the work of Freud in this area has had the effect of significantly complicating matters and muddying the waters in terms of whether accounts of childhood abuse are to be believed or not – see Ussher, 2011). We are now seeing greater emphasis on childhood trauma as a factor in adult mental health (Rogers & Pilgrim, 2005), as is evidenced not only by the professional literature, but also autobiographical accounts of childhood experience. For example, Gillett (2011) provides a moving and very insightful account of her experiences of child abuse and subsequent schizophrenia. *A Fine Line: A Balance to Survive* by Lisa W. B. (see http://www. afineline-lisawb.co.uk/) is also an important text in this regard.

It is important to recognise that there are two sides to the notion of whole-life effects. The first side is the direct lifelong effects on children who have been abused – that is, the recognition that children can carry the negative impact of the abuse with them throughout their lives. However, in addition to this psychological issue, there is the sociological issue of the cumulative effect of the negative impact of abuse, in so far as children who become abusers can go on to create considerable distress and trauma for other children, thereby widening significantly the negative impact of their own experiences of abuse. Similarly, where abuse leads to mental health problems in adulthood, this has a detrimental effect not only on the individuals concerned, but also on their loved ones and, indeed, often on wider society. The overall cumulative effect across the lifespan of abuse is therefore of major proportions.

The significance of loss

It would be remiss of us to discuss the horror of abuse without considering how loss features in the lives of children who have been abused. Loss and grief are features of everyone's life, but what can be particularly difficult to deal with are experiences of what are referred to as 'complicated grief' (Stroebe *et al*, 2012). Two significant forms of complicated grief are multiple and cumulative losses. Multiple losses are those that are experienced at the same time – for example, when an incident occurs which produces a number of losses. The trauma of abuse would clearly fall into this category – a child who has been abused will experience a wide range of losses, many of which will be experienced simultaneously. Consider the following, identified by Thompson (1999):

■ boundaries

■ trust

■ hope

■ feelings and what they mean

■ intimacy

■ childhood

■ spontaneity

■ privacy

■ self-respect

■ confidence and serenity

■ family

■ happiness

■ identity

(p116, drawing on the work of Stewart, 1994)

Cumulative losses are those which build up over time: one loss, then another, followed shortly by another and so on. This, too, can be seen as very significant for abused children because, while they will experience a range of losses when abuse is first instigated, there will be further losses over time that will produce the effect of cumulative loss. This combination of multiple and cumulative losses can be particularly devastating for a child. This devastation is, of course, consistent with the notion of the experience of trauma. Indeed, it can be seen that trauma is a form of loss, a particularly devastating form.

In terms of loss experiences, an important concept in this regard is that of disenfranchised grief (Doka, 2001). This refers to forms of grief that are not socially sanctioned, because, for example, the nature of the loss is not socially validated (death by suicide, for example). Losses that are not directly associated with death can also be disenfranchised in so far as it is often the case that people who are concerned with grief issues do not recognise grief in situations that do not involve bereavement (Thompson, 2012). That is, if a death has not occurred, then many people will not see the significance of grief. This is particularly significant in relation to the losses associated with abuse, which, if not recognised or given adequate attention, can be disenfranchised and can therefore add an additional layer of suffering for the person experiencing the losses concerned.

One consequence of disenfranchised grief is the absence of rituals. Rituals in the time of a significant loss can be very helpful in bringing people together to share their feelings and to provide important social support (and thereby provide a platform for developing ontological security). Rituals can also help to provide frameworks of meaning at a time when meaning has been disrupted by the significant loss. Where the losses are associated with abuse, rather than with death, it is unlikely that there will be any form of ritual to help the person concerned engage with other people in a meaningful and supportive way. This is an important issue for recovery, and is therefore something we will consider further in Chapter 5.

There is much more that could be said about the significance of loss in relation to child abuse and trauma. Indeed, it could form the basis of a book in its own right. However, we should have provided a sufficiently strong argument to show that loss is a factor that we need to take very seriously when we are working with children who have encountered the horror of abuse.

Conclusion

This chapter has been quite wide ranging, and has addressed a significant number of ways in which the horror of abuse can have detrimental effects on children. It has therefore emphasised just how destructive a force abuse can be in the lives of children and as a destructive force as a social problem more broadly.

What is perhaps particularly significant about the horror of abuse is that so many abuse situations boil down to children needing protection from the people who should be their primary protectors. The immense vulnerability that arises from protectors becoming abusers is, tragically, at the heart of much of the abuse that features as part of contemporary society.

Looking closely at the horror of abuse and its impact can be a dispiriting experience. However, all is not lost. There are steps that can be taken to minimise or avoid these effects. The whole idea of recovery from trauma is indeed premised on the commitment to making a positive difference in this regard. It is therefore to this topic that we return in the following chapter.

Chapter 5: The importance of recovery

Introduction

This chapter revisits the central theme of recovery in order to explore the key issues in more depth and detail. The fundamental point that we wish to emphasise here is that trauma does not have to be a life sentence – there are steps that can be taken to bring about at least a degree of recovery. Although, by its very nature, trauma is a devastating experience, our focus in this chapter is on the range of ways and means of addressing the problems it presents and enabling the people affected by it to move forward positively wherever possible.

Developments in neuroscience have helped us to understand what is happening in the body (in the brain and nervous system in particular) when a person encounters a traumatic experience. It has been established that early life traumas can lead to a form of brain damage, in the sense that the brain's development and function can be adversely affected (for example, Ziegler, 2002). However, we should not allow that to lead us to the pessimistic conclusion that improvements cannot be made. Experience has shown that new neural pathways can be developed with appropriate intervention (Van der Kolk, 2015), as the work of Mary and her team has shown. In other words, although it is true to say that trauma can be damaging at a physiological level, it is important to recognise that that damage can be undone in certain circumstances – it is not necessarily permanent.

The process of recovery from trauma is not a simple or straightforward one, and so this chapter explores some of the complexities involved and helps to establish a firm foundation of understanding, so that practitioners involved in working with abused and traumatised children have a sound basis on which to develop their practice.

The chapter takes the form of responses to a set of questions, namely:

- What is recovery?
- What is happening in recovery?
- How do we promote recovery?

- What can prevent recovery?
- And, finally, how long does recovery take?

We shall address each of these in turn.

What is recovery?

Bentovim *et al* (2009) make the important point that: 'The core task for professionals where a child or young person has experienced significant harm is to assist them and their families or their carers in their journey to recovery' (p11). This helps to establish how significant recovery is as a basis for working with abused and traumatised children, and so it is important that we are about clear what we mean by recovery. Unless we begin with a clear foundation of understanding there is a danger that there will be scope for confusion and misunderstanding.

Key point

Well-informed practitioners can make hugely positive contributions to the quality of life of traumatised children, while ill-informed interventions can prove highly problematic and counterproductive. It is therefore essential that there is clarity about what is involved in promoting recovery.

Beyond a medical model

While there is now much greater awareness of the significance of trauma in the lives of abused children, there is still a considerable need to develop our awareness and understanding further. One obstacle to developing a greater understanding is the danger of uncritically adopting a simplistic medical model, of taking terms like 'recovery' and 'healing' too literally, as if recovering from a medical condition. To adopt a medical model of trauma, rather than a holistic psychosocial one, is dangerous because it:

1. Pathologises individuals – that is, it presents the problem as if it were something wrong *within* the individual, and can thus reinforce a sense of shame or stigma. This can in effect add insult to injury, making the situation worse. As Tomlinson (2004) acknowledges, we have to be careful about the language we use in relation to traumatised children. This returns us to the important theme of meaning, as language is, of course, a fundamental element of how we create and sustain meanings.

2. Fails to consider the important role of wider social factors, such as interpersonal relationships and the influence of cultural and structural issues (the significance of diversity, for example (Robinson & Jones Diaz, 2006)). A medical model draws attention away from the wider picture and is therefore not sufficiently holistic – it does not do justice to the complexities involved. Neglecting the role of wider socio-political factors can lead to too narrow a perspective that does not give us an adequate picture of the range of issues involved, as we shall discuss in more detail in Chapter 7.

In a similar vein, Briere (1992) makes an important point:

'The notion that abuse-related behavior is not reflective of illness potentially increases the survivor's sense of self-control (as opposed to control by a disease process), and removes the stigma inherent in being defined in terms of pathology. Sadly, clinicians who adhere to a medical model when working with abuse survivors can do the reverse: by referring to 'symptoms' and 'disorders' when describing abuse sequelae, they can further complicate or intensify client stigmatisation.'
(p126)

Interestingly, while Briere makes a valid and important point in arguing against the use of medical terminology, the use of the term 'sequelae' is also unhelpful, as it unnecessarily mystifies what is involved. Sequelae is simply a technical term for 'consequences', but the use of technical jargon that excludes many people who are not familiar with it in place of perfectly adequate everyday terms, serves as an obstacle to understanding, not an aid to it.

While medicalised approaches to psychosocial issues are increasingly being criticised (Bracken & Thomas, 2005; Crossley, 2006; Thompson, 2019a), representing progress in the developing sophistication of the theory base, scientific advances in neurobiology in relation to trauma have produced a number of texts that adopt an oversimplified approach that relies on biological reductionism (Rothschild, 2006; Solomon & Siegel, 2003; Ziegler, 2002) – that is, an approach that presents complex multi-level psychosocial phenomena as if they were single-level issues, as simply matters of biology.

While, with a physical wound, an element of healing is expected to take place before we can say that a person has 'recovered' from their physical trauma, much the same can be said of a psychosocial trauma. What is happening in effect is that a metaphorical process of healing is leading to a situation where we can, we hope, ultimately claim that the person concerned has achieved recovery (but see below for an important discussion about the timeline involved in recovery).

Healing

'Healing' means making whole again, and so it is quite an appropriate term in referring to the physical healing of a physical wound, but it is also very appropriate in terms of the spiritual healing of a spiritual wound, where a child's identity and their sense of how they fit into the world has been challenged and disrupted. The notion of spirituality is therefore a key aspect of recovery. It is important to re-emphasise here the point made earlier that spirituality does not necessarily mean religion. Not all people are religious, but, of course, everybody has spiritual needs and challenges, children included – and especially abused children whose sense of security has been undermined by abuse. Spirituality gives us our sense of identity, of who we are, how we fit into the world and, in particular, it answers our question: am I safe? Spirituality gives us what Moss (2005) calls a 'worldview'. Our sense of spirituality will shape how we perceive the world and ourselves as part of it. It therefore follows that our sense of whether we are safe or not is part of that worldview. We can therefore recognise that a key part of recovery is the task of establishing a sense of safety or, to return to the discussion in Chapter 4, a strong sense of ontological security (see page 87).

Thompson (2009) comments on the distinction Schiraldi (1999) makes between healing and recovery:

'Healing refers to initial stages where we begin to come to terms with what has happened. It is our initial step after going through the abyss of trauma. It is what we begin to do when we come out the other side. Recovery, by contrast, refers to the longer term process of putting our lives back in order and trying to move away from the harm done psychologically and socially to us.'
(p63)

This fits with the notion of recovery as an idea of rebuilding, reconstructing our lives after trauma has devastated it in some way. This can be extremely difficult even for mature, competent adults with an extensive support network, but for children who have yet to learn many of life's lessons, especially children who have little by way of a support network, can find this exceptionally difficult and challenging. What is therefore involved in promoting recovery, to a large extent, is assisting in the rebuilding of a meaningful life, one that is not rooted in fear and distress. We shall return to this point below.

No standard patterns

We can recognise a number of recurring themes across the recovery process, but it is essential that we realise that this does not amount to standard patterns. It is certainly not the case that children recover from trauma in a standard way. It is not a matter of simply finding a cure for the ailment, as it were. Good practice dictates that there needs to be a detailed assessment of how the trauma has devastated the child, across what range of indicators, and, indeed, as discussed in Chapter 2, this is what the Mary Walsh Approach is based on. However, for now it is important to recognise that, while it is wise to have a good understanding of common themes in recovery, this is no substitute for having a clear picture of the specific circumstances of the individual child concerned. A 'one size fits all' approach will be far from adequate and risks making the situation worse in some ways. This again emphasises the importance of assessment, of gathering sufficient information to develop a meaningful picture of the child's life and current circumstances, the risks involved and so on.

When a child has worked through and come to terms with what has happened to them, we could be forgiven for believing that they had recovered. And sometimes that is true. However, more often life events trigger past experiences and the original trauma will need to be addressed again. These events might be their first sexual experience, their first breakup, marriage, the birth of their first child, menopause and so on. It may be more helpful to think about recovery as a process, a journey that may not have a destination per se.

It is also important to be aware that recovery involves more than containment. It is unfortunately the case that, for many years, it was thought that it was acceptable simply to 'look after' children, for example by providing alternative home accommodation for them and attending to their basic needs (as 'corporate parents'). As we have noted, there was a common but false assumption that if abused children were given adequate care and attention, they would 'get over' their traumatic experience. We are now quite clear that that is not the case and that failing to address trauma risks considerable further difficulties for the children and their carers. One of the findings of the Waterhouse investigation into abuse in residential childcare (aptly titled *Lost in Care* (Waterhouse, 2000)) expressed concern about the tendency that had developed for children simply to be 'warehoused', as if there was an underlying assumption that they would grow out of their difficulties. The notion of recovery builds on this to recognise that caring for children is certainly better than simply warehousing them, but also to acknowledge that simply addressing their basic needs – although very important – is not sufficient in and of itself.

'Containment' in the sense of emotional holding is, of course, a good thing, an important part of rebuilding a sound foundation of emotional security, as we shall explore in more detail shortly. However, containment in the sense of simply warehousing children is actually likely to undermine their sense of security, and particularly their sense of self-worth when they consistently receive messages to the effect that their specific needs are not being addressed.

What is happening in recovery?

We shall explore in more detail below the Mary Walsh Approach to promoting recovery, and that discussion will highlight the particular elements involved. However, for now it is important to recognise some important themes that relate to the process of recovery. We shall outline some of the main ones, three in particular: emotional holding, meaning reconstruction and developing resilience.

Emotional holding

A key theme here is, of course, that of emotional holding, helping to create an environment where the child feels safe from immediate danger, so that a longer-lasting sense of safety and (ontological) security can be developed. We noted earlier that 'holding' is a metaphorical term that refers to engaging with a child in ways that produce a similar positive impact to that of physically holding someone (for example by giving them a reassuring hug). Holding, in the sense we are using it here, can certainly incorporate that – touch, when used appropriately, is a very important form of non-verbal communication and human interaction. But we also need to recognise that it is much more than just physical holding. It involves creating an atmosphere in which the child feels able to talk openly and freely without fear of being made to feel guilty or ashamed. Indeed, it needs to be made clear to the child that there is no need for them to feel guilty or ashamed – feeling 'dirty', as many abused children have referred to it over the years. It involves creating a sense of basic care and comfort, but more than this, it involves creating a sense that this is a place where feelings can be expressed, directly or indirectly, and will not be used as a weapon against the child (for example, in the form of a punishment).

This process of holding helps to establish a baseline of 'connection' – that is, a foundation from which the child can make meaningful connections with other children and with supportive adults. It provides a baseline from which progress can be developed and measured. A key part of this is the development of new attachments. We noted in Chapter 3 that attachment difficulties are often associated with abuse. Helping children to form new, strong, meaningful, secure attachments is therefore a fundamental part of recovery. It helps to create a sense of safety through having supportive connections with people who will be able to help them withstand their pressures and their trials and tribulations.

Meaning reconstruction

Once holding has been used effectively to help create such a foundation of connection, there is the potential for what is known technically as 'meaning reconstruction' (Neimeyer, 2010), as discussed earlier (see p73). The idea of meaning reconstruction is that, when a person has experienced a profound loss (including traumatic losses), they lose meaning. If someone dies, the grieving person loses not only someone important to them, but also a set of meanings, a framework that has helped them make sense of their lives. For example, if a parent loses a child, their whole sense of what it means to be a parent can be disrupted.

But the process does not just relate to bereavement situations. Someone who has been abused is likely to lose their willingness to trust people. They then have to adjust to understanding the world in new ways (that is, develop new meanings) which reflect the implications of no longer trusting people. Grieving can therefore be understood as a painful process characterised by the need to develop new meanings to help make sense of the world that has been so severely disrupted by loss.

This is closely linked to the idea of narrative therapy (Payne, 2006; Harms, 2018), which is based on the idea that people who have had traumatic experiences can be skilfully helped to develop new frameworks of meaning (narratives) that are more positive and empowering for them. As we noted in Chapter 3, this can be an important way of helping children to move away from a narrative of being a helpless victim, through to being an active survivor, and on to a more positive sense of being a person made whole again, a person renewed – healed and therefore well on the way to recovery.

Life story work is clearly a central plank of this, but it is important to understand that the whole process of recovery is in itself one of meaning reconstruction, of developing a new narrative that tells a different story from one of helplessness and powerlessness, and constructs one premised on a degree of control, confidence and connection (to adults who can be trusted).

Key point

Meaning and how it is shaped and reshaped by life experiences is such a central part of our lives that there is a tendency for us to take it for granted and not pay it the attention it deserves. Being effective in promoting recovery therefore involves becoming more 'tuned in' to meanings and their role in influencing our experience and our quality of life.

Developing resilience

Resilience refers to the ability to 'bounce back' from adversity. It is an important part of an individual's psychological make up and is particularly important for children who face problems – including the problems associated with trauma. Daniel and Wassell (2002) helpfully describe three factors that can be seen to underpin resilience:

1. A secure base which helps to create a sense of belonging and security (note the link with attachment theory).

2. A high level of self-esteem that brings an internal sense of worth and competence.

3. A sense of self-efficacy that involves a degree of mastery and control, accompanied by an accurate understanding of both one's personal strengths and limitations.

The same authors argue that: 'The concept of resilience increasingly offers an alternative framework for intervention, the focus being on the assessment of potential areas of strength within the child's whole system' (2002, p13). This fits well with what has come to be known as the 'strengths perspective' (Desai, 2018; Saleebey, 2008), which is based on the idea that traditional approaches to helping people deal with problems has tended to focus on the negatives and paid relatively little attention to the strengths that can be drawn upon in seeking to tackle problems. It has therefore sought to balance out the traditional focus on negatives with a greater degree of attention paid to the positives that can easily get missed by practitioners focusing on the negative. A balanced approach that takes account of both the risks, problems and challenges as well as the strengths and protective factors is therefore what is needed when it comes to promoting recovery.

Promoting resilience can be seen as an important contribution to helping children recover from trauma. It is not enough for adults to provide care and protection; efforts also have to be made to reinforce the child's strengths in respect of resilience – for example, by providing unconditional support. This can be very important in rebuilding a sense of trust and security.

Developing resilience is not, however, a simple or straightforward matter. Hosin casts light on this by commenting on how variable the circumstances can be in relation to resilience:

'We are differently resilient under different conditions. Some of the factors that influence our resilience are individual, and some are social and cultural. People who are and remain socially competent and autonomous in the situation which

they find themselves, able to apply thinking skills and problem solving ability creatively, and able to maintain a sense of perspective and humour are more likely to be resilient in the face of trauma. If we can retain a sense of overarching moral order, of meaning and purpose, and of spiritual values, we are more able to stay centred and healthy when exposed to the disintegrative chaos of traumatic stress. And people who are held in a network of close, confiding relationships with positive and secure attachments are much more resilient in the face of potentially overwhelming stress.'
(2007, p191)

There are some key points in this passage that are worth highlighting:

- **Social and cultural factors**. The need to go beyond individualism is again being emphasised. If we regard resilience as simply a personal characteristic, there is a danger that individuals become pathologised due to the significance of wider socio-political issues not being taken into consideration (Thompson & Cox, 2020).

- **A sense of perspective**. Adults can play an important role in helping children keep things in proportion. Young imaginations can run wild, while balanced support from an understanding adult can help to prevent perspective being lost.

- **Meaning and purpose**. Again, the importance of meaning appears as a key theme. Purpose or a sense of direction is also part of this picture, and once again this brings us back to the importance of spirituality, which stresses the importance of meaning and purpose as underpinnings of a sense of spiritual well-being.

- **A network of close, confiding relationships**. Adults have an important part to play in developing such a network. Children who find it difficult to trust are likely to operate in a very small network, and so building up a fuller network of supportive adults who can be trusted is an important part of the process.

- **Positive and secure attachments**. This reinforces the importance of understanding and strengthening attachments. Without secure attachments, trust will not be rebuilt and a future adult life of mistrust, fear, suspicion and disconnection will be the likely result.

It is also essential to remember that development is not a simple 'unilinear' process. This applies in two senses:

1. There are various 'strands' or elements of development, primarily the following:
   a. Cognitive – concerned with thought processes, reasoning and memory.
   b. Emotional – concerned with emotional responses and expression.

c. Social – how the individual is influenced by, and contributes to, the wider social sphere.

d. Moral – how children learn right from wrong and learn about cultural values.

e. Political – how children learn to use (and resist) power.

f. Ontological – concerned with rising to the existential challenges life throws at us (for example, learning to cope with separation).

It would therefore be a mistake to fail to recognise that a child may be developing at different rates along different dimensions. For example, a child who is well developed socially may nonetheless be less well developed emotionally, quite possibly to a significant extent when abuse and trauma are involved.

2. Progress is not always 'neat', in the sense that gains can at times be lost and there can be plateaus during which there is little or no development for a while. It is the overall picture, across time and circumstance, that should inform our interventions (see the discussion of assessment below).

Figure 5.1: Three aspects of what happens in recovery

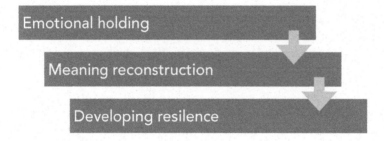

Emotional holding

Meaning reconstruction

Developing resilence

Key point

Child development is a complex, multi-dimensional matter. It is not necessary for recovery practitioners to be experts in this field, but at least a basic understanding of the key issues involved is needed, and the more thorough the knowledge the better. Everyday 'folk wisdom' ideas about child development can be misleading and unhelpful.

How do we promote recovery?

In Chapter 2 we saw that the Mary Walsh Approach to recovery involves the integration of three elements: individual therapy, life story work and therapeutic parenting. Each of these has an important part to play in developing the holding (and the foundation of connection it brings) that will in turn allow the seeds of new attachments to take root and flourish into new narratives of empowerment and recovery. We will now revisit these three core elements of the integrated model to identify how they play a role in bringing about change, and also reflect briefly on the associated outcomes and assessment framework.

Individual therapy

Rogers (1960), somewhat arrogantly, describes therapy as the process of giving birth to a new personality. Our thinking has moved on since then and now recognises that it is a matter of a new way of making sense of our lives that is needed and not a new personality as such. However, a child's identity is a very important part of what needs to be considered in terms of trauma recovery, but a much fuller, less atomistic understanding of identity is called for. As Rymaszewska and Philpot comment:

*'The formation of our sense of self, of our identity, is complicated and delicate.
Critical to it is our ability to form mature, loving and trusting relationships
with others. Our ability to do that is shaped very much in our earliest years.
This attachment is what is lacking for those whose experience of trauma, loss and
abuse ruptures the process. Therapy seeks to restore it.'*
(2006, pp50-51)

Individual therapy is geared towards promoting recovery by helping the child to express feelings, grieve losses, build trust, find hope and reframe negative experiences. As such, it has a central role to play in the recovery process. A positive relationship with a trusted, skilled and reliable therapist is an important ingredient. As Thomas and Philpot helpfully explain:

*'By making use, for example, of techniques like play, music, art, dance and drama,
the therapist can help the child slowly examine some of the harmful experiences
of her past. It is the task of the therapist to assist the child in unravelling her
confused and overwhelming feelings, containing her as she does so, and help her to
externalize those feelings so that they cease to have power over her.'*
(2009, p53)

In effect, individual therapy creates a safe space for the child to grow, to move away from the negative experiences and build a safer, more positive experience of life.

Life story work

The narrative emphasis of life story work can be particularly helpful. By reviewing early life experiences and making sense of them, the child is helped to develop a more positive framework of meaning, an empowering narrative that provides a solid foundation for the child to move forward with their life, leaving the traumatic experience behind in some ways. Rose and Philpot make apt comment when they explain that:

'The life story worker picks up the shattered shards of a child's life, putting them together with great sensitivity. A long process begins to help children internalize understandings and to explore the meaning of their life and identity. Without the opportunity to integrate this work into the rest of the therapeutic task, the chances of children being able to make sense of what has happened to them and put the past into place are very slim.'
(2005, p10)

The process is therefore very much one of meaning reconstruction, with the individual therapy helping to create the safe space within which this reconstruction can take place.

Life story work is not an easy option, but it is an important one. It serves as a platform for clearing up confusion (and the anxiety that it can bring) and for developing new understandings that are essential to recovery. As Rose (2012) argued, the value and power of a life story approach to reconstructing and reconnecting a child through personal narrative should not be underestimated.

Therapeutic parenting

Parenting any child is a challenging business. Parenting a child who has been traumatised and who is having difficulties in regulating their emotions (and associated behaviours) is, of course, significantly more challenging. It is therefore essential that foster carers and residential child care staff receive appropriate training and support (see Chapter 8). Without this, vicious circles can develop in which carers are pushed to their limits (and quite possibly beyond) and may therefore respond to the child in unhelpful ways. As Pughe and Philpot clarify:

'Children should not feel that they are being punished for their neglect or the damage they cause. Rather they should be given to understand that their carers see this as a communication to be understood and given meaning. However, this can be easier said than done. It is no easy thing for carers to retain their understanding of why some children act negatively and attack the very home

which the carers try to look after – and this can often happen day in and day out for lengthy periods.'
(2007, p57)

If traumatised children are not being parented in ways that reflect an understanding of the often extreme demands that are placed on carers in such circumstances, the result can be harmful not only for the children themselves, but also for the adult carers (and, indeed, in fostering situations, for the foster carers' own children).

There therefore needs to be clarity about what is needed to provide a therapeutic parenting context for abused children. Pughe and Philpot refer to what Maginn calls seven 'pillars of parenting' for those who work with children and young people in care. These 'pillars' fit very well with the idea of therapeutic parenting. They are:

■ primary care and protection

■ secure attachment

■ positive self-perception

■ emotional competence

■ self-management skills

■ resilience

■ a sense of belonging.

(Pugh & Philpot, 2007, pp33-4)

These can form a useful platform for developing therapeutic parenting as a key part of an integrated, holistic approach to trauma recovery.

Outcomes

Linked to these three elements are the set of outcomes (highlighted in Chapter 2) that help to give a clear picture of the progress being made in terms of recovery. This means that the notion of recovery is not just a vague one of generally having an improved situation. The specific outcomes provide a much more useful framework for pinning down exact aspects of the child's situation in terms of whether or not progress is being made. This can be a very helpful basis for ensuring that professionals are clear about which issues need attention and which do not.

Without a focus on a specific set of outcomes and some way of identifying whether or not they are being achieved, there is a significant danger of drift – that is, a loss of focus that can be detrimental to the child. Where there are clear, explicit outcomes to work towards everyone involved is in a stronger position to move forward and to be aware of what is working and what is not. The use of such outcomes is a major strength of the Mary Walsh Approach.

No doubt the best outcome is when a child or young person can say: 'Yes, that happened to me, it was horrible, but it no longer has the power to affect how I think, feel and behave'. They can go into adulthood, ready to take their place in society and bring up their own children safely.

Assessment

In addition we should not forget the Mary Walsh assessment model (also discussed in Chapter 2), with its six aspects that can also be measured in terms of progress. This helps to answer the question of how we can promote recovery, but also gives us some significant clues about another related question: how do we measure recovery?

Assessment should, of course, not be a simple matter of gathering information and ticking boxes. Children being looked after away from their family of origin are likely to benefit from having (and contributing to) a thorough assessment (Horwath, 2010). For children who are being looked after because of abuse and trauma, the need for detailed, skilled and insightful assessment can be seen to be even higher. Assessment is crucial because it provides an overview of the situation, identifies key factors (needs, strengths, risks and so on) and helps us to develop a meaningful plan for making a positive difference.

Key point

The central role of assessment in all work with children cannot be overestimated. Trying to bring about change without a thorough and detailed knowledge of the child's needs and circumstances, the risks they face, the experiences they have had and their wishes and feelings is potentially a very dangerous undertaking. In situations involving abuse and trauma it is especially risky, and so we need to be entirely clear that there can be no substitute for a proper assessment.

What can prevent recovery?

It has to be recognised that there are various things that can get in the way of successful recovery. Perhaps one of the most important of these is the influence of wider social issues. Important factors, such as poverty and deprivation, unemployment and social alienation or disaffection can lead to a profound sense of hopelessness and listlessness (these are important enough to justify a chapter of their own – Chapter 7). These, in turn, can reinforce low self-esteem and associated problems. In such circumstances, it is not surprising that many people will turn to recreational drugs as a form of escapism. Parents who do this can then become emotionally unavailable to their children. This, in turn, can lead to attachment problems, leaving the child to be influenced by other children who are, in effect, helping to meet their attachment needs. Where this happens in environments in which there are high levels of crime and violence and drug use, the net result can be children who become part of a culture of hopelessness and escapism characterised by the use of drugs. This in turn can lead to a very strong sense of spiritual impoverishment. There can be a denial of a sense of purpose and direction or belonging. This can lead to disaffection and alienation, feeling that they do not belong within society. This can then produce disinhibition, which in turn can result in anti-social behaviour, more serious crime, very dangerous, potentially life-threatening use of illegal substances and, of course, the abuse of vulnerable people, whether adults or children.

This scenario of a high level of social problems in certain areas presents great difficulties in terms of the challenges of social policy to address the well-being of a society's citizens (Thompson, 2017b). Where children have been brought up in such environments, there can be much that can stand in the way of their developing a positive identity, high self-esteem and a sense of security and stability. Many children who have been removed from such environments have been helped to grow and develop, and their return to such environments does not necessarily mean that they are doomed to return to their previously problematic state. However, it does have to be recognised that the challenges they face are very significant indeed.

> ## Practice focus 5.1
>
> Becky was 13 when staff at her school noticed that she was behaving oddly. They alerted the authorities and during the police interview she described long-term sexual abuse at the hands of her stepfather. In order to avoid prosecution, he poured petrol over himself and set himself on fire, in front of Becky. Becky was severely traumatised as a result of these experiences and could not tolerate talking or even thinking about what had happened. She started taking drugs to blank out her memories. She blamed herself for her stepfather's death and her family blamed her, too. She had spasmodic bouts of violent flashbacks and she was self-harming, her arms streaked with scars and her hands full of cigarette burns. As she moved into adulthood these episodes became more psychotic.

Another issue that can prevent recovery is the traditional reliance on therapy alone. Mary Walsh in particular has been at pains to emphasise the need for a holistic, integrated approach. As Mary has acknowledged (quoted in Chapter 2), an emphasis on therapy alone can be dangerous and disempowering. Therapy needs to be part of the much broader approach that also incorporates life story work and therapeutic parenting.

A third important factor that can seriously stand in the way of recovery is the behaviour of the child concerned. There is sadly a very real danger that a vicious circle can develop in which the demanding and challenging behaviour of an abused and traumatised child can lead to people who may be able to help them backing off and not feeling able to offer any meaningful support. Children displaying challenging behaviour can be very difficult to reach, potentially leading to a continuation of such behaviour. It has to be acknowledged that helping such troubled children can indeed be very troubling in itself and takes a great amount of perseverance, courage and commitment. Success in this area can never be guaranteed. We shall return to this point in Chapter 8 where the importance of staff support is given due attention.

Figure 5.2: Obstacles to recovery

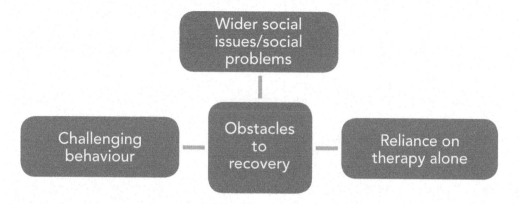

How long does recovery take?

There is no simple, straightforward answer to this question, other than: 'as long as it takes'. This is because, in a sense, recovery is a lifelong matter. The point was made earlier that trauma is a form of loss, and it has long been recognised that we never fully get over a major loss. For example, Stroebe and Schut (1999) present a dual process model of grieving that shows how people can oscillate between a 'restoration orientation' (where they are focusing on rebuilding their life after their loss) and a 'loss orientation' (which involves focusing on the loss itself, on whom or what has been lost). Their theory helps us to understand that grieving is a process that involves swinging between these two extremes. Gradually, over time, we will spend more time in restoration orientation, but there is always the possibility, even years after a significant loss, of returning to a loss orientation, albeit briefly.

We can see here a strong parallel in terms of recovering from trauma, but the expectation is not that the child will reach a point where they will never ever again be troubled by any memories of their traumatic experience. That would be to ask too much. However, it is realistic to expect that, with appropriate help, children can be supported to reach a point where they are spending the vast majority of their time in 'restoration orientation', and that they are therefore in a position to live fulfilling lives, no longer victims of the entrapment that traumatic experiences entail.

How long it will take a particular individual to reach that stage will vary significantly, and so it really is the case that there is no simple answer to the question of how long recovery takes. We should, though, be fully aware that we are more likely to be talking about years than weeks or months. For this reason it is important that early intervention is offered wherever possible. Indeed, the sooner that help can be forthcoming, the more effective it is likely to be, given the fact that experiences of trauma can, in effect, eat away at self-esteem and a child's sense of hope that anything can be done to alleviate their difficulties and rescue them from their ordeal.

One important implication of the fact that recovery is likely to be a longer-term process is the importance of tracking. It should be helpful for organisations working with abused and traumatised children to develop a system whereby they can monitor progress, so that there is an overall picture of what helps and what does not. Indeed, the significance of evidence-based practice has long been a hallmark of the current governmental and organisational approach and is now receiving much stronger attention (Bentovim *et al*, 2009; Pozzulo & Bennell, 2019).

Key point

In terms of timescales we need to get the balance right. We need to avoid being impatient and expecting positive results to emerge quickly, while also not writing off children when progress is slow. Every child will work at their own pace and there will be considerable variation across any group of children. Good and impressive progress can at times be made very quickly, but consolidating and building on that progress can take much longer.

Conclusion

Recovery is a term that is difficult to define and pin down, but the discussions in this chapter should have helped to make clear that it is nonetheless a vitally important concept, and one that merits considerable investment of time, effort and resources in order to maximise the potential of efforts geared towards promoting recovery. In essence, recovery is a process of helping children to learn that not all adults are abusive and that, by trusting those adults who are not abusive, significant progress can be made in moving away from the harm done by the tragic devastation of the damaging actions of perpetrators of abuse.

Earlier approaches to dealing with children who had been abused tended, as already noted, to neglect the significance and long-lasting effects of trauma. One of the implications of neglecting trauma has also been the neglect of the positive potential of trauma. While trauma, due to its extremely destructive qualities, is of course not something to be encouraged, it would be a significant missed opportunity to fail to recognise that trauma also offers the potential for growth and development. As Tomlinson puts it: 'Trauma is an experience that potentially can be recovered from and even made use of' (2004, p16). This is consistent with the work of a growing group of scholars who recognise the value of what has come to be known as 'post-traumatic growth' (Calhoun & Tedeschi, 1999; Harvey, 2002). It is an idea closely associated with transformational grief – that is, grief that is not just lived through and left behind, but rather, grief that has the effect of bringing about positive change. As Schneider recognised: 'Transformative potential is created when we can reassess what we have lost and discover an internal richness never appreciated before ... discovering innocence through renewal and forgiveness' (1994, p14).

Schneider also points out that, while grieving is a universal human response to loss, the potential to grow from it is not always recognised and, moreover, that potential can be lost as a result of such factors as oppression (Schneider, 2000). Abuse can, of course, be just such a form of oppression.

The aim of recovery and healing, then, is not simply putting traumatised children back together again, or 'restitution'. Rather, it is a process of helping put children on track for maximising their potential, for helping them use the experience as a point of growth. The Walsh Recovery Programme is geared towards releasing as much of that potential as possible.

Chapter 6: Being child centred

Introduction

A key feature of the Mary Walsh Approach has been to recognise the crucial need to be child centred. Indeed, being child centred needs to be recognised as a fundamental value underpinning all work with children, but especially with those children who have been traumatised by abuse. Unfortunately, some people misunderstand the notion of being child centred and interpret it to mean being indulgent towards children. This is certainly not what is meant by the notion of being child centred, as being indulgent would not be helpful to a child. Rather, it is a case of recognising that, in the busy, pressurised contemporary world in which we live, it is very easy for relatively powerless children to go unheard, for their voice not to feature among the competing demands for attention, resources and assistance. This is clearly not helpful when it comes to helping children recover from the trauma associated with abuse. What is needed, then, is a firm commitment to being child centred in our approach to helping children. As Mary herself has put it (in the foreword to Rymaszewska and Philpot): 'We respect unconditionally the child's process and we believe in keeping the child at the centre of everything that we do' (2006, p11). The importance of developing that respect is what this chapter is all about.

The idea of being child centred can be seen as a matter of encouraging self-mastery and self-efficacy, important aspects of growing up for all children, but especially so for children who have had such disruptive and disempowering experiences as abuse and trauma. It involves encouraging children to take ownership for themselves, their lives and their feelings (with appropriate adult support, of course). It helps to encourage a higher level of self-esteem through an internal locus of control – that is, where they recognise the extent to which they can have a say in shaping their own circumstances. Someone with an external locus of control, by contrast, is a person who does not recognise their own ability to make a difference – trauma can encourage the adoption of an external locus of control, a form of self-disempowerment. High self-esteem and an internal locus of control can be encouraged and reinforced, and thereby challenge any sense of guilt or self-blame.

Being child centred has now come to be recognised as an important part of working with children in any professional context. In the past, the idea that children should be seen and not heard caused considerable problems in terms of marginalising children and young people – not only disempowering them, but also making them more prone to being abused due to the vulnerability involved. This traditional view can therefore be seen to have, in part at least, contributed to the persistence of abuse, owing to the fact that children's voices were silenced by cultural convention. Giving children a voice is therefore not only a powerful weapon when it comes to preventing abuse, but also an important part of the process of recovery. This is because, if children are to be able to recover from traumatic experiences of abuse, they have to feel that it is safe to reveal their feelings and that what they have to say will be listened to and taken seriously and not used against them in any way.

Practice focus 6.1

Jason was the eldest of five children who were all removed from their parents for gross neglect. Jason and his sister Liz were placed together in foster care. They had been in care for a couple of years but lately their foster mother was anxious as she was aware that there was some sexualised behaviour between the two children. I was asked to do an assessment in relation to Jason and went to see him at his foster home. When we met I said: 'Hello, my name is Mary and I talk to lots of children who have a touching problem'.

'I've got a touching problem, it happened when I was at home, my dad threw me down the stairs, he didn't give us any food, he made me have cold baths with my brothers, he locked me in a cupboard with spiders in it and he rubbed my willy till it was sore and he made me rub his till the white stuff came out.'

Despite the fact that he had been in care for some time, he had never spoken before of his abuse, until I made myself relevant to him.

It is important to note that being child centred does not mean abdicating your adult role. There are times when it is important that decisions are made on behalf of children, as a parent might do, but these should be made in the best interests of the child, and not because it is the easiest solution for the adults.

Values-driven practice

To understand the notion of being child centred, it is important to put it in the context of a value base. The caring professions as a whole share certain values in terms of such principles as confidentiality, treating people with dignity and respect, a commitment to promoting equality and valuing diversity, and so on. When it comes to working with children, we should also add being child centred as a fundamental value. That is, it should be seen not simply as a technique or method in a technical sense, but rather as something more fundamental than that – a commitment to the ethical principle that children have a right to be heard and adults have no right to silence them without good cause. It can therefore be helpful to understand child-centred practice as part of this wider picture of professional values.

This value has its roots, in part, in the United Nations Convention on the Rights of the Child[1] This has been quite an influential document that has made a significant difference at a number of levels. However, it is not only as a result of such legislative or policy developments that our value base has been extended. The notion of ageism and the need for anti-ageist practice has been a growing trend in adult services work in recent years (Thompson, 2019b). The need to avoid discriminating against older people is now firmly on the agenda of the professional education of social workers, nurses and so on. There has been a spin off from this, insofar as the growth of awareness of, and interest in, ageism in relation to older people has begun to influence professional practice and education in relation to children.

For example, the work of Thompson (2005) focuses mainly on the sadly very common experience of discrimination in the lives of older people, but also makes the important point that discrimination can apply to children and young people as well. As she explains:

'...it would be easy to think of ageism as relating solely to the experiences of older people ... However, we should not forget those at the opposite end of the age spectrum. It is not unusual for children and adolescents to be discriminated against on the grounds of their age, too, and to be treated less favourably than adults whose voices are more powerful and whose right to have those voices heard is accepted more readily.'
(2005, p1)

This recognition that ageism applies to discrimination against people on the grounds of age at any stage in the life course helps us to locate the value of being child centred in the context of anti-discriminatory practice more broadly. Indeed, the importance of valuing diversity relates to children as much as it does to adults. It can be seen to apply in two ways: first, children will – like any other group of people – come from diverse backgrounds, and so all that we have learned about the importance of valuing diversity in recent years applies to children just as much as it does to adults.

---

1   https://www.unicef.org.uk/what-we-do/un-convention-child-rights/ (accessed June 2019)

Second, we need to recognise that age itself is a form of diversity. That is, it is a way in which different groups of people can be characterised and therefore potentially discriminated against. As part of this, we need to recognise the importance of individuality without individualism. What we mean by this is that, as Thompson (2018c) explains, we are all unique individuals, but we are unique individuals in a social context. The recognition that we are all unique individuals is our individuality. The recognition that individuality operates within a social context means that we need to go beyond individualism (or what is often referred to as 'atomism'). That is, we need to avoid the error of assuming that, because we are all unique individuals, there is no wider social context that we need to consider. Children as a group face considerable potential for being discriminated against. This discrimination often manifests itself in the form of their voice not being heard, or their needs being regarded as secondary. When it comes, as mentioned earlier, to competing voices, the relatively powerless voices of children can be ineffective if adults do not make space for taking on board the views of children.

If we neglect these basic facts, we run the risk of not only being ineffective, but also contributing yet further to discrimination against a vulnerable and relatively defenceless section of the population. Being child centred is therefore an important part of developing anti-discriminatory practice as part of a broadly humanitarian approach.

Giving children a voice

There has been a growth of literature over the years that relates to the importance of recognizing the value of listening to children and giving them a voice (for example, Boylan & Dalrymple, 2009; Percy-Smith & Thomas, 2009). A theme throughout this literature has been the recognition that there are skills involved in being able to encourage children to have their say and to, in a sense, give them permission to do so, to challenge the dominant cultural assumption that children should only speak when spoken to.

We shall return below to the issue of skills involved in listening to children, but for now it is important to emphasise that it is a matter that needs to be taken seriously and given appropriate attention. If not, then there is a danger that lip service is paid to the idea of genuinely listening to children without it actually happening in any meaningful way. For example, the established patterns of not tuning in to children and taking on board what they are saying may continue without people even realising that they are marginalising children and young people.

Adams goes a step further in arguing that, while there has been a growing emphasis on listening to children, there is still a tendency not to hear the spiritual voice of the child. She argues that there is the possibility that listening to children can become part of policy in education and child welfare circles without genuinely connecting with a child's spiritual concerns:

'The increasing strength of the child's voice in many formal and informal social contexts lies in stark contrast to their spiritual voice which is often silenced, resulting in children's fear of a negative response. Yet the spiritual is a vital element of a child's education, allowing them to explore their inner life, find their place in the world and seek answers to the "big" questions in life, either within a religious context or outside of it.'
(2009, p120)

We would add that it is a vital part of not only education, but also recovery from trauma.

This lack of emphasis on the spiritual perhaps reflects the broader tendency for spiritual matters to be neglected in the caring professions (Holloway & Moss, 2010), something which the Mary Walsh Approach has been aware of, and has provided a counterbalance to, through its emphasis on a holistic, integrated approach that fully recognises that spirituality is a key part of the child's reality.

Mary's approach has also shown a genuine commitment to giving children a voice through the development of a children's council in the residential settings she had been involved in setting up. By encouraging children to get involved in making decisions about the running of their home, they were empowered to learn how to exercise authority responsibly, how to speak their mind in a way that is constructive and to learn important lessons for adult life. It was Mary's intention that the council should enable children to recognise that not all people in authority are abusive, and it proved very successful in this regard. Mary was delighted on one occasion to overhear one child telling another that Mary was the boss but she was not bossy. What pleased her about this comment was that it was made in the context of the children's council and confirmed to her that her approach was working in the sense that the children recognised that she was indeed an authority figure, but one who still allowed them to have their voice, to have their say in matters that were important to them. The same child went on to say: 'She really listens to us'. In other words, they recognised that she had a degree of power, but had no intention of abusing that power – an important lesson for children who have suffered abuse as a result of one or more adults abusing their power over them.

This is just one way in which efforts can be made to ensure that children's voices are heard, that they are given the opportunity to express their views and feelings and not feel that they have to keep them bottled up.

What can so easily stand in the way of children being listened to is not so much any lack of concern or interest on the part of staff, but the pressures of work they face. The 'adult noise' of working life, with all its various demands and challenges, can easily drown out the voice of the child unintentionally. It is therefore essential that people working with children bear this in mind and make every effort to ensure that, however loud that adult noise gets, it must not be allowed to silence children. Indeed, not hearing the voice of the child can make our work harder and therefore add to that adult noise.

An important factor to consider in terms of giving children a voice is that it needs to be balanced against professional insights. People often talk of the expertise of the client needing to be acknowledged, but Back challenges this view. He relates how he was once listening to a presentation at a conference:

'A respected professor of sociology stood up and said boldly: 'the people are the experts in their own lives!' There was a murmur in the audience, not necessarily one of approval. I thought to myself, 'Hmm ... sounds good, nice radical gesture – the people are the experts in their own lives'. I started to think more carefully and came to a realisation: being a professor of sociology is no necessary protection from saying utterly stupid things. If the people were experts in their own lives, love affairs would never end, we would never make mistakes, nor do things that injured our interest or did us harm. I am certainly not an expert in my own life, and who amongst us could make such a claim?'
(2007, p9)

It is important to recognise that the people we seek to help in the caring professions, whether adults or children, are often in a state of confusion and are not necessarily experts in their own circumstances. They will, of course, have a degree of knowledge and understanding (which we may label 'expertise') of their own experience, but the term 'expert' has much broader implications than this. Similarly, professionals should not be seen as the experts if, by this, it is meant the people with the 'answers'. The basis of partnership working is that professionals and their clientele work together in a spirit of shared endeavour to reach agreed outcomes. This is what is involved in the idea of giving children a voice, that they should be part of that partnership. They should not be excluded from having a say in what happens to them simply because of their age or developmental level. To exclude them on the grounds of age would be a form of discrimination, as highlighted earlier.

While a degree of professional expertise is indeed called for, it needs to be acknowledged and understood that not all professionals will necessarily adopt a child-centred approach. For example, Mary recounts the case of a child who was not being listened to in the process of court proceedings relating to her until, through Mary's own intervention in the form of a report to the court and oral testimony relating to that report, the child's perspective could begin to be taken into account. As Mary put it: 'To be able to give the child directly a voice in court was a joy actually. It was another skill learned really' – and what an important skill that has turned out to be.

Key point

Working in partnership is fundamental to high-quality child care practice. It is not simply about working collaboratively with other professionals or forming an effective rapport with parents; it is also, fundamentally, about making sure that we have meaningful connections with the children concerned – that is a key part of being child centred (just as being child centred is a key part of working in partnership).

Figure 6.1: Working in partnership

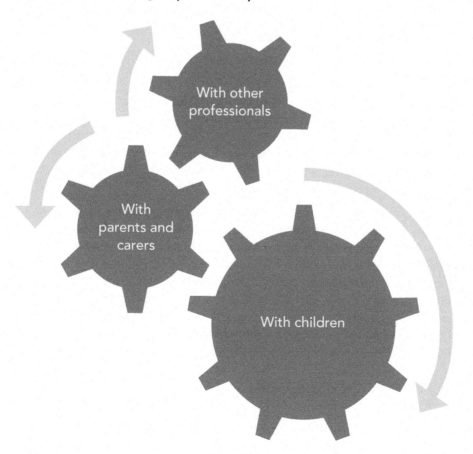

The art of listening

This is a term that highlights the skilled nature of listening to children. The idea of giving children a voice is not simply that of listening in the conventional sense; it involves much more than that. It involves being able to engage with children in a meaningful way, especially when they are having difficulty communicating, whether that difficulty arises from their age or developmental level or from the difficult nature of their experience (for example, talking about abusive experiences).

Mary Walsh has become a pioneer in the use of toys to communicate effectively with children. The toy box approach has been the subject of a great deal of training over the years in helping people from a wide range of organisations to learn the skills involved in communicating non-verbally about difficult topics with children who are not able to communicate in other ways or at other levels. This approach has been a major feature of the innovative nature of the Mary Walsh Approach. It is a powerful way of creating an environment where the child feels comfortable enough and safe enough to address complex, painful issues in meaningful ways without being at all distressed or unnerved by the process.

Practice focus 6.2

I was asked to do an assessment of a four-year old girl for care proceedings. She had been sexually abused, but there were three possible perpetrators and Rosie was frightened to say who it was who abused her. The children's guardian (Guardian ad litem) was afraid that there was insufficient evidence and Rosie may have had to be returned home, where she would be at even greater risk. She had been through police interviews and said nothing

In our first session with the toybox she seemed really scared, but she was curious about the toys. Eventually she came and explored my toy box. She picked up all the dolls one by one and pulled their pants down. I noticed what she was doing and commented that she was looking for something special. She said that she was and then showed me with a little girl doll that was being sexually molested by a male doll. She named the little girl doll Rosie and the male doll her stepfather, Bill. So, instead of firing questions at her which would have driven her into a frightened silence, I created a safe space where she was free to explore what she was frightened about. The court made the care order as a result of this work

---

Whether communicating through the toy box method or in other ways, it is vitally important that the adult goes at the child's pace. Trying to push a child into communicating when they are not ready for it could be, at the very least, counterproductive and, in some circumstances, potentially abusive in its own right, creating emotional distress for a child who already has more than enough to deal with in terms of complex, intense emotional challenges. Having the patience and understanding to work at the child's pace may be difficult for some people especially, but the sacrifices involved are likely to prove very worthwhile. This is because working at the child's pace gives them a very important message to the effect that we are genuinely concerned about them, that they can trust us, that we have their interests at heart and that they do not have to rush on our account. This is likely to produce much more positive and helpful results than impatiently trying to pressurise (whether gently or otherwise) a child into communicating at a pace that we feel more comfortable with, or which suits our own time pressures.

Similarly, we need to be aware of the need to communicate with a child at an appropriate developmental level. For example, how we talk to a four-year old and a 14-year old is likely to be very different, in terms of their levels of understanding, their expectations of interpersonal interactions and the communicative styles they will feel comfortable with. We therefore have to draw on the knowledge of child development that is expected of all child care professionals, but to take this to a slightly more advanced level in terms of the specifics of communication as they relate to emotionally sensitive issues in relation to abuse and trauma.

If we get this wrong and attempt to communicate at a level that is not appropriate to a child's developmental understanding, then we may discourage them from communicating with us, and thereby create unnecessary barriers. It is important to emphasise that the focus needs to be on *developmental level* rather than age. This is because many children who have been abused will be operating at a developmental level below their chronological age. To be misguided by the age of a child into assuming that they have a degree of understanding and development that in fact they have yet to achieve can be highly problematic.

> ## Key point
>
> Beware of being misled by a child's level of linguistic development. Some children will be able to speak at quite an advanced level, showing very good linguistic skills, but not have reached a similar level of intellectual or emotional development. Similarly, at the other end of the spectrum, some children will have achieved a limited level of linguistic development that will make it harder for them to express their feelings, hence the importance once again of non-verbal communication at a level appropriate to the child's development.

Finally, in relation to the art of listening, it is worth mentioning the Aboriginal concept of Dadirri listening. This refers to the ancient wisdom of recognising the importance of listening not only with our ears but also with our heart, a 'deep' listening. This is a recognition that listening has to be at a spiritual level, in the sense of making a real connection with the person concerned. It fits well with Buber's (2013) notion of relating to people in terms of I-Thou, rather than I-it – that is, interacting in ways that recognise the humanity of the other person and therefore treating them with respect and concern (I-Thou), rather than relating to others in purely instrumental ways (I-it), that dehumanise both parties in the transaction. Dadirri listening involves being able to make a meaningful connection with the person concerned, genuinely to connect, person to person, and not simply have a mechanistic approach to listening to children.

The child's reality

If we are to enable children to move on in their lives and get past the problems presented by having been abused and traumatised, then we have to be able to understand their perception of the world. It is the child's reality that counts, in the sense that that is what will be governing their approach to their life. The technical term for this is 'phenomenology', which literally means the study of perception (phenomenon literally means 'that which is perceived'). Phenomenology is a theoretical concept that enables us to recognise the importance of appreciating the child's reality. This is because people will respond to situations as they perceive them, whether that perception is accurate or not. For example, if someone is under the impression they are in danger, the fear they will feel will be real (and will therefore influence their behaviour and their reactions to the situation and the people in it), even if they are not actually in any danger at that particular moment. The fact that there is no 'real' danger does not mean that the fear is not real.

Gadamer, a major figure in the development of phenomenological theory, described how everyone views the world from their own particular viewpoint, their 'horizon', as he called it (Gadamer, 2004). He also wrote of the 'fusion of horizons', the way in which, for communication, interaction and understanding to take place, different people with different viewpoints need to come together to appreciate one another's perspective, hence the notion of a 'fusion' of horizons. Genuinely listening to a child involves just such a fusion – it is not simply a matter of paying attention in an everyday sense. It involves an element of imagination, being able to put ourselves in another person's shoes, as it were, so that we can have a better understanding of how they see the situation, a better way of seeing 'where they are coming from'.

Simply saying that a child's perception has been distorted by abuse is unhelpful, as it oversimplifies a complex situation and implies that the child is somehow 'wrong' to see the situation in a certain way – another example of the danger of pathologising, locating the problem within the individual and not appreciating the nuances of the wider context. That distortion, however it may appear to an outsider, is the child's reality and that is what will be governing their behaviour and their emotional and cognitive responses, as well as their level of spiritual well-being. Being child centred therefore means that we have to have a genuine appreciation of that child's reality, to be able, as the saying goes, to 'walk a mile in their moccasins'. If we are not able to do that we will fail to connect with the child, fail to hear what they are saying, and therefore fail to be child centred.

This does not mean that we should not challenge any distortions that do arise. In fact, that is a key part of recovery, but it needs to be done skilfully, at the appropriate pace and at the appropriate time, rather than clumsily by simply telling a child that they are wrong in how they perceive a situation in particular or their life in general. In other words, we have to help them to rewrite that narrative, rather than simply dismiss it as the 'wrong' narrative.

Key point

The way children and adults see the world and make sense of it will often be radically different, and we need to be aware of that. But we also have to be aware that each child's perspective and understanding will be unique, no doubt having certain things in common with other children, but nonetheless distinctive to the individual child.

One important aspect of this relates to the concept of the myth of 'wonderful children'. This is a term that derives from the work of Ong (1985), who has written about how it can be a factor in child abuse for parents to have a very romantic view of having a child. They can expect that, when they become parents, all their difficulties will be resolved because they will have a wonderful child in whom they can invest all their love and concern, and who will love them back. When they are then faced with what can be a very harsh reality – a reality in which the demands of caring for a vulnerable young life has a significant impact on their own life – it can be very significant in terms of, for example, a young mother with her own unmet emotional needs who becomes pregnant and expects that having a baby will meet her needs. That having a child to invest her love in will make her feel loved and valued in return is perhaps, superficially, a reasonable expectation, but in reality it is a highly problematic one, because it fails to recognise that bringing up children is very hard, demanding work that involves a lot of sacrifices. This can be very demanding for anyone, but for people who have their own emotional issues to resolve and their own unmet needs to address, it can be especially problematic.

This can result in situations where the mother may, for example, objectify the baby as part of herself. Her desire to receive satisfaction of her own needs through the baby can lead her to see the baby as, in a sense, an extension of herself. If those unmet needs of the mother result (or emanate from) low self-esteem or even self-loathing, the mother may harm the baby as a form of self-harm. It is not uncommon, for example, for people who have low self-esteem to the point of self-hatred, to self-harm. If the baby is perceived by the mother as an extension of herself, then harming the baby will have a similar, if tragic, effect.

This idea is well captured by a situation she encountered many times: a young girl, say 15 or 16, feels that her needs have never been met, so she becomes pregnant; the father is out of the picture, and so before long she is on her own with a baby. Her thoughts can easily turn to ideas along the line of: 'Nobody has loved me in all my life, this baby will love me. I will be the sun and moon' and other such idealizations. After she has had the baby she realizes that the situation is not what she had expected, but she then objectifies the baby as part of herself. It is no longer a baby, it is part of her. 'I hate myself', she thinks, and so it does not matter if I hit the baby, because the baby part of me.

Howe also discusses how pressures on parents can be a significant part of how abusive situations develop:

'Faced with a needy, vulnerable or distressed child, the maltreating parent feels disorganized, out-of-control, and without a strategy to deal with his or her own

emotional arousal, or that of his or her child. The result is abuse, neglect or both.' (2005, pp5-6)

There may well also be a generational dimension to this, in the sense that many children who are not well cared for and have attachment problems are more likely to have difficulties in being good parents when they reach adulthood. However, it is important to emphasise that this is not the same as saying people who have had negative experiences of being parented will necessarily become poor parents in turn. The reality is much more complex than this. As mentioned earlier, some people who have had negative experiences of being parented subsequently becoming excellent parents because they are determined to give their child(ren) a much better start in life than they had.

This is an example of why it is important to adopt a phenomenological approach – to see the situation from the point of view of the person(s) concerned and not overgeneralise or seek to adopt a 'one size fits all' approach. In understanding the development of abuse through Ong's concept of the myth of wonderful children, in particular, and many parents being ill-equipped to deal with the major demands of parenthood, we can understand how the parents' own sense of reality can be problematic. For children who have been abused, a similar process can occur, and how they perceive their reality may be largely coloured by experiences of mistrust, exploitation and immense confusion. If we are not attuned to that reality and to how significant these perceptions are, then we will fail to connect with that child or young person. We will therefore not have any right to describe our practice as child centred, and it is highly unlikely that we will make any progress in helping the child to move forward positively.

In sum, then, an understanding of the child's reality needs to be a fundamental part of working in partnership. If we do not address these matters sensitively, our practice can boil down to trying to persuade the child to see things our way, something they are likely to be unwilling or unable to do – and, of course, something that is unlikely to be helpful even if it were to be achieved.

Key point

We need to bear in mind that each of us will have our own sense of reality, our own worldview. It can be very helpful to be aware of what that is, of what assumptions we are making, and on what values, principles or beliefs we are basing our actions, decisions and emotional responses, as these may be highly significant in terms of how we are approaching our work. A reasonable level of self-awareness is therefore something we should aim for.

Active participation

In Chapter 3 we discussed the importance of having a balanced approach to hope. Giving children hope, and building on any hope they may already have, involves listening to children, giving them a voice so that they can play an active part in their recovery and build up resilience in the process. In this vein, Wyness warns us against seeing children as passive recipients of 'treatment': 'to emphasise children's passivity is to marginalise and trivialise any attempts that children might make to fight back' (2006, p20). We would also argue that being child centred means not only listening to children and appreciating their reality, but also supporting them in being actively engaged in the process of recovery, being active participants. That is, being child centred involves a focus on empowerment – helping children gain greater control over their lives.

If we are to understand empowerment we must first understand power (Thompson, 2007). Bannister (2003) is correct in linking child abuse to the abuse of power. She is also correct in placing an emphasis on empowering children. The following comment is particularly important:

'...child abuse is always an abuse of power ... children remain powerless in most situations: in society, in the family and in school. Children often lack a voice, and adults may not know how to communicate with them. To empower children, to give them a voice, must be our aim.'
(2003, p77)

Indeed, putting children at the heart of the enterprise, helping their voice to be heard and helping to create an atmosphere in which they are safe to air their views and feelings is a vital part of the Walsh Recovery Programme and what it stands for. Tomlinson and Philpot (2008) reinforce the importance of this:

'As Kane (2007) reminds us, 'research suggests that listening and really involving children and young people is key to effective care planning'. Timms and Thoburn (2002) say the same thing when they say, "experience tells us that plans have a better chance of success where the children themselves have been involved in their preparation".'
(2008, p109)

Empowering children means moving away from the traditional idea that children are 'adults in waiting' and will get their chance to participate in due course, but are not yet ready for any meaningful involvement – active agents and citizens of the future, but not of the present. This traditional view has been challenged by what McDonald refers to as 'the new sociology of childhood'. She offers a useful insight:

'The new sociology of childhood not only allows us to appreciate the logic (and ethics) of attending to the present, it also allows us to do so in that it emphasises the competence of children as social actors and as informants about their lives. Children are 'keen, constructive and thoughtful commentators on their everyday lives at home, at school and in the wider community' and as such, have a richness of knowledge to offer that would be senseless to neglect (Prout, 2002: 71).' (2009, p12)

Active participation does not mean ignoring children's needs and any vulnerability factors that are likely to arise due to their immaturity and the development they have yet to achieve, but it does mean not allowing such matters to serve as a basis for failing to give children a voice and allow them to have a say in their future.

Figure 6.2: Active participation

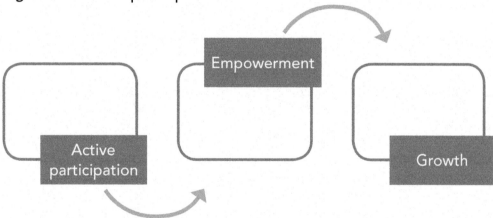

Key point

Traditional notions of treatment imply that it is something that happens *to* the recipient, while the more holistic integrated Walsh Recovery System is based on a more empowering model of *active participation*. Conceiving therapy as something that is done to children in a pseudomedical sense runs counter to the idea of being child centred and actively involving the child in their process of recovery.

Conclusion

If we return for a moment to the main theme of Chapter 5, that of recovery, we should now be able to see why being child centred is so important. If we are to work in partnership with a child in navigating their way through very distressing, unpleasant, even terrifying, waters, then we have to give them a very clear message that we understand where they are coming from, that we 'speak their language', and perhaps most importantly of all, that we are listening to what they are saying because we genuinely want to help. We have already commented on more than one occasion about the dangers of secrecy and denial. Being child centred is an important antidote to secrecy and denial. By being child centred, by being open, honest and transparent, we are not allowing any collusion with such secrecy and denial. We are helping the child to recognise that, while they are indeed in a very difficult and demanding, painful place, we are aware of this and we are fully prepared to support them in moving out of that dangerous, hostile place into one of relative security.

If we are not genuinely committed to being child centred, we will not be able to form the meaningful connections that are a part of partnership working, and so our efforts will be fruitless. This means that we will be playing a part in condemning a child to staying in a very difficult place, rather than being an important, positive part of helping the child to move forward positively and constructively.

Being child centred with this generation of children should also help to prevent problems for the next. A young parent may think: 'If my needs are not being met, I cannot meet my children's needs, and so they may well grow up with their needs not being met, thereby increasing the risk that they will then neglect their children's needs, thereby initiating – or perpetuating – a vicious circle of stress and distress. This makes it all the more important that we take seriously our commitment to being child centred.

Chapter 7: Equality, diversity and inclusion

Introduction

Early theoretical understandings of trauma were rooted in psychodynamic theory, while more recent developments in our understanding owe much to progress made in the field of neuropsychology. Both these schools of thought have added significantly and helpfully to our understanding of trauma. However, both are largely individualistic in their focus. We have argued previously (Thompson & Walsh, 2010; Walsh & Thompson, 2017) that these insights need to be complemented by a broader sociological approach to take fuller account of wider cultural and structural issues that can have a major bearing on the circumstances leading to abuse; how abuse is defined, conceptualised and reported in the media; how its consequences are managed (by the individuals concerned and by members of the helping professions).

This chapter therefore seeks to counterbalance the individualistic emphasis by highlighting a number of wider sociological factors that can also be seen to be relevant to our understanding of childhood trauma and the abuse that gives rise to it. In particular, we will be emphasising the significance of discrimination in the context of equality, diversity and inclusion.

Defining our terms

For a very long time the caring professions paid little or no attention to discrimination and its impact on the people they were supporting. However, that all changed in the 1980s when a major focus on discrimination and oppression developed. This initially led to a defensive and oversimplified approach that failed to do justice to the subtleties and complexities involved (see Thompson (2018c) for a discussion of this), quickly evolving into what became known as the 'political correctness' approach. This approach focused on changing the language used to avoid discriminatory terminology being used (for example, changing chairman to chair to avoid reinforcing the sexist idea that positions of power belong to men).

The focus on language was to be welcomed, as much discrimination operates through this medium. However, these are complex matters, and so simply banning certain words and replacing them with others (often with no explanation as to why) was never going to be enough to bring about the necessary change.

Instead of promoting the sensitivity to language that was needed, the political correctness approach at best made people feel anxious about what were and what were not 'PC' terms, and at worst alienated people from the need to make changes to the language used – that is, they rejected the approach as 'PC nonsense' (Thompson, 2018a). Consequently, an opportunity was missed to appreciate the fundamental role of language in reflecting and reinforcing underlying structures of inequality and disadvantage.

Key point

Issues relating to discrimination and its impact have tended to be either ignored or dealt with in a simplistic way at times in the past. We need to learn the lessons from the past and ensure that we remain aware that issues of discrimination are complex and sensitive and therefore need to be handled accordingly.

Because of this unfortunate history of issues of discrimination first being ignored and subsequently dealt with in very superficial and simplistic ways, we want to make sure that in this chapter we are doing justice to the complexity of the issues involved. Part of this is to be clear about the key terms we are using.

Equality

First of all, it is important to move away from the idea that equality means sameness. In its literal sense, equality can be understood to mean sameness (if two people are paid an equal amount of money, for example, this means they are receiving the same amount of money). However, in its moral, professional or political sense, equality should not be reduced to the idea of sameness (Witcher, 2013).

What can be much more helpful is to think of equality as equal fairness, not simply as uniformity. At times it will be fair to treat everybody the same – for example, participants on a training course all being given the same length of coffee break. However, there are times when it is fair to treat people differently because of different needs or circumstances. For example, if one of the participants on the training course needed urgent medical attention, it would be fair for him or her to receive it, while the others who do not need it do not receive any such medical treatment. The key issue is fairness, not sameness. Where sameness comes into the equation is the importance of everyone having an equal right to be treated fairly.

In this way, equality can be understood as the absence of discrimination. As we shall see below, to be discriminated against means to be treated unfairly. Equality is the opposite of this; it is about having the same right as everyone else to be treated fairly and without prejudice.

Mistakenly assuming that promoting equality means treating everybody the same is potentially highly problematic. For example, if we interpret equality for disabled people as treating them the same as we treat everybody else, then that is likely to add to discrimination, rather than reduce or eliminate it. Consider access to buildings, for example. If we were to treat, say, wheelchair users the same way we treat people who do not use a wheelchair, it would be sufficient to provide steps or stairs and not provide lifts or ramps. Clearly, wheelchair users would be disadvantaged by being treated 'the same' as everyone else. Equality is about equal fairness, not about sameness.

We can apply the same logic to working with traumatised children. If we adopt the simplistic mantra of 'We believe in equality, we believe in treating everybody the same', then the specific needs of such children will not be addressed.

To avoid confusion, some people use the term 'equity' in place of equality to emphasise that it is not about sameness. However, this too can be confusing, as so much literature, including law and policy documents, exists that uses 'equality' in our sense of equal fairness. But whichever term we use, we need to remember that our emphasis needs to be on fairness, not sameness. This is partly why equality is so often associated with the notion of social justice, as the latter very much depends on the former (Barry, 2005).

Figure 7.1: Equality

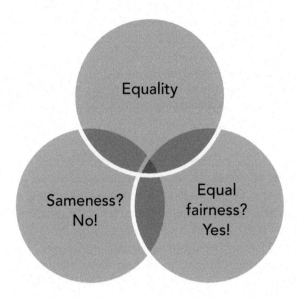

Diversity

Diversity is about variety; about the recognition that people come in different shapes and sizes, with different perspectives, different needs, different strengths and different problems. What has come to be known as the 'diversity approach' involves recognising two key principles (and their significance):

1. **We live and work in a diverse society**. There is a strong tendency (in the media, for example) to focus on what we have in common, and that is no bad thing in itself, of course. However, what it can do is draw attention away from our differences, to de-emphasise the variety across individuals and groups of people. What we have in society is a rich diversity of people, with each of us and the groups we represent contributing to what is often referred to as the 'kaleidoscope' of humanity. The idea that as people 'we are all the same' is not wrong by any means, but it only tells part of the story. The reality is this:

   a. In some ways we are all the same – in terms of biology, for example. If we are cut, we will bleed, regardless of who we are or where we come from.
   b. In some ways each of us is unique, with our own idiosyncratic characteristics, our own unique 'story' of our life. Even identical twins, who have so much in common, will have their own unique identity.

c. In some ways, some of us are the same and some of us are different. For example, people from the same culture will have much in common with one another, but there will be differences between them and members of a different culture.

It is this third element that is important in terms of diversity. It involves recognising that, despite our shared humanity, there will be often highly significant differences in terms of culture, gender, class, linguistic group, religion, ethnicity, nationality, political allegiance, sexual orientation and so on. Yes, we are all the same in one sense, we are all unique in another, but we must not neglect the significance of what sociologists call 'social divisions' – that is, the various groups and categories that each of us belongs to and which shape our understanding and experience of the world.

2. **Diversity is a good thing – it is an asset, not a problem.** Despite the fact that difference and diversity are a basic feature of social life, as we have just noted, there is an unfortunate tendency for difference to be seen as a problem, or even as a threat. An 'us-them' mentality is sadly very common. However, the diversity approach challenges this and presents difference and variety as positive things, as assets for us to benefit from. This is why we often talk of 'valuing diversity' or even 'celebrating diversity'. It is about recognising that variety enriches society and therefore our lives. Imagine how drab and unappealing life would be if everyone were the same, with the same tastes, opinions, attitudes, outlook and preferences. Imagine how impoverished we would be if we had little variety in the food we eat – just traditional staples, rather than the rich international and multicultural array of dishes so readily available these days. Think, too, about the variety of styles of music we have from different parts of the world and how impoverished we would be if all we had available to us was traditional folk music (however good that traditional folk music may be).

Key point

We need to move away from the idea that differences are necessarily a bad thing and embrace the recognition that they can also be very positive, offering variety and enrichment, providing different perspectives that we can learn from. Valuing diversity opens the door to greater tolerance and respect, innovation and learning.

What underpins the diversity approach is the idea that, if we focus on valuing diversity and thereby benefitting from the variety of perspectives and contributions different people make, there is far less likelihood of discrimination arising. For example, if having different groups from different cultures or ethnic backgrounds within a community is seen as an asset and an enrichment, there will be less racial discrimination. This is based on the idea that racism in large part stems from an attitude that, 'They are not like us, so they must be inferior to us or a threat to us, or both'. The diversity approach seeks to replace that attitude with one that recognises that being exposed to different cultures and outlooks enriches our life and does not threaten us in any way.

One important point to emphasise is that our focus on diversity needs to *complement* a focus on equality, and not replace it. Unfortunately, some people (who should know better) have been heard to say words to the effect of: 'We're not concerned with equality now, we are using the diversity approach', as if the latter somehow displaces the former. This is a dangerous assumption to make because it fails to recognise that equality and diversity are two sides of the same coin. If we want to value diversity, we need to make sure that everyone is treated fairly; if we want to make sure that everyone is treated fairly, we need to value diversity.

Inclusion

It is not at all uncommon for what are intended to be universal services, whether public or private, to focus on catering for the *majority* of people, rather than *all* people. To return to the example we gave earlier, buildings that have steps and/or stairs but no lifts or ramps are, in effect, excluding those members of the population who for whatever reason are not able to access the building. Another example would be documents that use dark print on a dark background, thereby excluding people with low vision.

But it is not simply a matter of disability. There are many other ways in which certain groups or categories of people are systematically excluded. For example, the tendency for children not to be consulted about various matters will generally have the effect of excluding them. Consider, for example, how many family holidays have been ruined by the parents deciding on the holiday arrangements without consulting their children and then having to contend with unsettled and discontented children.

This latter point is particularly relevant to working with children traumatised by abuse. This is for two reasons:

1. It is highly likely that, in the course of the abuse taking place, they will not have been listened to, and their wishes, needs and feelings will not have been considered because the needs of the perpetrator were taking precedence. In effect, the children will have been 'silenced' by the abuse, literally and

metaphorically, and so if we make the mistake of excluding them, we run the risk of creating unsettling echoes of the abuse for them.

2. As we noted in Chapter 1, one of the important values underpinning work with traumatised children is being child centred, and that very much hinges on being able and willing to listen to children and to include them wherever possible. We cannot expect to win children's trust (and thereby help them to relearn how to trust) if we are not including them and empowering them in the process.

It is important to stress that such exclusion is generally unintentional. It can at times be the case that there is a deliberate strategy of exclusion being used, but, for the most part, it is an unwitting exclusion rooted in habit and unthinking routines. This reflects the significance of power structures, as it is generally the least powerful people who tend to be excluded most. We shall return to the theme of power below.

Key point

The two key elements of inclusion are: (i) ensuring you include *everyone*, not just the *majority* of people; and (ii) ensuring you listen and involve people, especially children or other marginalised groups.

Discrimination

In its literal sense, to discriminate means to identify a difference. It is generally a positive and helpful thing – for example, to discriminate between edible foodstuffs and poison. However, what often happens is that people discriminate against another individual, group or category of people. That is, they not only identify one or more differences, but also go a step further by using such differences as the basis for treating others unfairly (hence the link between equality and discrimination mentioned earlier).

An example of this is sexism. Because men and women are different in a number of ways, these differences can be used in an attempt to justify women (and sometimes men) being treated less favourably. For example, unequal pay for women continues to be a problem, decades after equal pay legislation entered the statute books in the UK.

It is in this latter, negative sense that the term 'discrimination' has led to the call for anti-discriminatory practice (or 'anti-oppressive practice', reflecting the oppression that discrimination leads to) to be an essential foundation of practice across the caring professions (Thompson, 2016b).

Just as exclusion will generally be of an unintentional nature, most discrimination is unintentional. This is in the sense that, for every act of deliberate discrimination, there will be many more unwitting instances. This is because much discrimination arises from the language we use which will reflect common stereotypical and discriminatory assumptions. For example, the common idea that it is women's role to be the primary carers will lead to women having certain restrictions placed on their lives, while many men will be denied the opportunity to gain the satisfaction and rewards of being a primary carer.

It is therefore not enough to be 'non-discriminatory' (that is, to seek to ensure that we do not actively discriminate against anyone in our work roles); we also need to be anti-discriminatory (that is, to be aware of how common discriminatory assumptions are and be prepared to challenge them constructively).

Cultural expectations

Having clarified some key terms and, we hope, having established a foundation of understanding of the need to be 'tuned in' to issues of equality, diversity, inclusion and discrimination, we now want to focus on some important considerations that will affect our work with traumatised children, beginning with the significance of cultural expectations.

There are two sides to cultural expectations that we need to consider and remain alert to. The first is that we come from our own cultural perspective, and that perspective will be having a major impact on how we understand situations and how we react to them. Consider how white people will often refer to people from a minority ethnic group as 'ethnic', as if they have no ethnicity of their own, as if there are 'ordinary' people (the majority) and 'ethnic' people (the minority) are not. That is, they will fail to recognise that we all come from an ethnic background, we all have cultural roots that influence us and help shape who we are. Another example might be when people refer to someone as a person 'with an accent', without recognising that we all have an accent, but we become oblivious to our own cultural background (including our accent) because we are so close to it we take it for granted.

A key term here is 'ethnocentrism'. This refers to the tendency to not only see the world from the perspective of our own ethnicity or culture, but to assume that our own view is the correct or best view, and therefore to assume that other views, informed by other cultures, are inferior, flawed or just plain wrong. An example of this is manners. Different cultures have different ways of being polite and showing respect. It is therefore an easy (ethnocentric) mistake for someone from a culture where it is the norm to say please and thank you to describe someone from a different culture (where there are ways of expressing politeness other than saying please or thank you) as rude, impolite or even 'uncivilised'.

Key point

Beware of ignoring or not appreciating the values, assumptions, perspectives, preferences and unwritten rules that you bring with you from your own cultural background. Not being aware of how these are affecting how you see and react to a situation can leave you ill-equipped to deal with a complex situation in which there are different perspectives and assumptions.

The second way in which cultural expectations are significant is how they affect the other people you work with – immediate colleagues, professionals from other agencies and of course the children themselves. Being aware of the cultural perspective of the other person, whether child or adult, can help to avoid unnecessary conflicts and misunderstandings.

Taking account of cultural differences can help us avoid two separate but related sets of problems:

1. If you are working with someone from the same (or similar) cultural background to yourself, you can end up with collusion. That is, you reinforce one another's worldview and thereby restrict your focus, possibly omitting consideration of an important aspect of the situation. This can also block learning, as we can become too comfortable in our ways of working, unwilling to stretch ourselves and go beyond our comfort zone.

2. If you are working with someone from a different cultural background from your own (including class differences), there is a danger that you can offend the other person, create unnecessary conflicts, misunderstand a key aspect of the situation and thereby create barriers to progress. This is particularly important in working with a traumatised child who is likely have trust issues. If you come across someone who is deeply embedded in your own cultural worldview and not open to embracing or at least appreciating a different worldview, then you are creating additional barriers to trust, not removing existing ones.

We should also note that, when a child feels different because of cultural differences, disability or sexual orientation, that difference becomes the focus of their abuse – for example, 'I am being abused because I am black/in a wheelchair/gay'. We need to be especially careful to address these distortions when working with these children.

> ## Key point
>
> Cultures can be defined as shared meanings, assumptions that are taken for granted and unwritten rules. They have a profound influence on us, and part of what makes them so influential is that we are largely unaware of how they are affecting us because we have grown so accustomed to them over the years. A culture provides a lens through which we see the world, and that lens will often be different from other people's lenses, so we need to consider how our own lens is affecting us and how other people's lenses are affecting them.

Alienation

To be alienated means to be treated as 'other', as different, in a negative sense. It involves being devalued and treated as a second-class citizen and often entails being excluded unfairly. It is associated with a range of social problems, especially in relation to mental health difficulties (Thompson, 2019). The groups or categories of people who are most prone to being discriminated against are also the people who are most likely to be alienated – the two processes generally go hand in hand.

Children who have been traumatised by abuse will also often experience alienation. Their experiences can lead them to see themselves (and for others to see them) as 'other' or as 'different', but not in a positive way. This can reinforce the sense of guilt and shame so often associated with having been abused.

This concept of alienation can therefore be an important and useful one in working with traumatised children. It can help us to bear in mind how it feels to be treated as 'other', as 'not one of us', as 'odd', and therefore not belonging or being valued. This can happen to children at school, in the community and even in their own family. Unfortunately, alienation has the potential to create a vicious circle:

Step 1: A child is abused and feels guilty and ashamed because of it.
Step 2: The child picks up signals from others that they are 'not normal', and this reinforces their sense of guilt and shame.

Step 3: This has the effect of undermining their self-esteem and reducing confidence.

Step 4: This can hamper the child's process of recovery.

Step 5: The child feels trapped and unable to escape the impact of the abuse.

Step 6: This makes them feel more alienated and their behaviour can lead to others alienating them by again seeing them as 'odd' or 'not normal'.

Part of recovery from trauma therefore needs to include being aware of, and prepared to address, the impact of alienation and the processes that give rise to it.

Gender and sexuality

For many years it was assumed by a significant proportion of people that victims of abuse were female and perpetrators were male. However, the situation is not that simple. It can be a significant mistake to assume that women are not capable of abusing. While it may be more likely for the perpetrator to be male, this is a far cry from assuming that all abusers are male. Both of the present authors have come across situations where there was a significant and damaging delay in addressing abuse because the perpetrator was female, and it therefore took longer to reach the conclusion that abuse was occurring – the idea of a woman committing abusive acts did not fit with the expected picture, and so the reality of the abusive situation took longer to discover.

Likewise, it is a serious mistake to assume that it is only girls who are sexually abused, as that means that abuse against boys may be similarly delayed in coming to light. Boys can be sexually abused by women, by men and by other boys, or indeed by girls in some cases, and so it is important that we do not exclude these possibilities from our thinking because we are operating on the basis of gender stereotypes about abuse and about sexual behaviour.

It is also important to consider sexual orientation and societal attitudes towards same-sex relationships. Although attitudes have mellowed in recent years and discrimination against lesbian and gay people has lessened, it would be a significant and costly mistake to assume that the problem has gone away. One of the implications of this is that children who have been abused by someone of the same sex can face additional distress because of the (unjustified) stigma associated with same-sex relationships and the potential for bullying because of this. The stigma can be internalised and add to the sense of guilt and shame, making it even harder to deal with.

It is very common, if not universal, for children to struggle to make sense of sexuality as they grow up, but this struggle can be strongly amplified by being exposed to adult sexuality before they are emotionally ready for it (and, in many cases, before they are physically ready for it). Complications over social attitudes towards same-sex relationships can add further to the struggle to make sense of what is happening.

Practice focus 7.1

Steve was nine when he came to SACCS. He had been abused by his father who also took him to sex parties where he was raped by several other men. He had very low self-esteem and was continually trying to hurt himself, by banging his head and also cutting himself. He believed that he was abused because he was gay and therefore it was his fault. In therapy, Steve was able to explore his experiences and his sexuality.

Because he was abused by men, he mistakenly assumed he must be gay. He was helped to see that, when the time came, he was free to choose his sexuality.

In a very real sense, this is a spiritual matter. This is because sexuality is a central part of who we are and how we fit into the world, of our worldview and of how we relate to other people. It affects the meanings we ascribe to our life experiences and therefore, potentially at least, our sense of direction.

Gender and sexuality, then, and the social meanings associated with them, can be understood as important issues that prompt us to look beyond the individual and take account of the wider social factors that can and so often do play a key role in our lives and in the lives of the children we are seeking to help through a process of recovery from trauma.

Key point

Issues relating to gender and sexuality are complex matters that reflect the wider social world, including processes of discrimination and alienation. We have to be careful not to oversimplify them and fall back on gender stereotypes or simplistic (and potentially discriminatory) approaches to sexuality.

Power

It has often been said that sexual abuse is not about sex, it is about power. However, when we examine that statement closely, we soon realise that it is far from the truth. This is not to say that power is not part of the scenario – indeed, it plays a central role. What we do need to recognise is that it makes no sense to say that sexual abuse is not about sex. A more accurate and helpful statement, therefore, would be that sexual abuse is not *only* about sex, but also about power. Indeed, the two – power and sex – are closely interlinked.

Since ancient times rape has been used as a weapon of war and, tragically, continues to be so to this day in some contexts. It is a way of expressing, and benefitting from, dominance. And, of course, sexuality – particularly sexual attractiveness – is regularly used as a power play, enabling people to get what they want, or at least making it more likely that they will do so. The links between power and sex are therefore manifold and complex.

Practice focus 7.2

I was asked to do an assessment on three children who were a boy aged eight and two girls, seven and five. Their father was very violent to them and to their mother. She was frequently locked outside the house and had no idea what was going on inside. She had now left him and was living alone with the children. What came to light during the assessment was that their father had raped all his children on a regular basis and this had started when they were babies. The children were in terror and feared for their lives. Until he was arrested they were too frightened to go with their mother to the shops in case they bumped into him and they wouldn't even go out to play.

Sexual behaviour involving consenting adults could be regarded as the authentic use of sexuality, whereas what we encounter when it comes to sexual abuse is what could be termed 'inauthentic sexuality'. It is when one party has been ether physically coerced, emotionally pressured or manipulated into engaging in sexual activity. Indeed, this is what makes it abuse – it is both power and abuse that are being abused, at the expense of the child.

One of the features of abuse-related trauma is sexualised behaviour on the part of the child. This will, of course, be due to learned behaviour to a certain extent – that is, the child will have come to see such encounters as a 'normal' basis for interaction. However, we can also see that there will be a power dimension at work here. Power relations are not static. They move and shift and reconfigure. So someone who is in a subordinate position in one context can become the dominant person in another context. Bullying is a sad but good example of this – a child who is bullied by an older sibling may then bully a younger sibling, someone further down the pecking order.

A similar process can occur in relation to abuse. A certain proportion of children who have been abused will go on to become perpetrators of abuse, either as adults or while still children (although we should be careful not to overestimate the prevalence of this phenomenon and assume – as some people have – that a child who has been abused is likely to go on to become an abuser).

In addition, if we return to our earlier consideration of key terms, we can see that power is implicated in each of them:

- **Equality**. A lack of fairness is very frequently associated with the (deliberate) abuse or (unwitting) misuse of power. The person who holds power – for example, by virtue of being an adult, especially an adult in a position of authority – is in a position of trust, and so being unfair towards other, less powerful people is an abuse of that trust.

- **Diversity**. Failing to value diversity and instead seeing groups or categories of people who are different in one or more ways from ourselves as inferior or as a threat also implicates power, in the sense that it is generally the majority (who hold greater power by virtue of being a majority) who are viewing less powerful minority groups as inferior or as a threat.

- **Inclusion**. A similar argument can be seen to apply. It is generally the least powerful factions who are being excluded, and the most powerful who are playing a leading role in excluding them. Or, at least, it is the cultural assumptions and the structural relations that serve the interests of the most powerful that create an ideology that serves to exclude certain groups or categories of people. For example, the idea that poverty arises as a result of the laziness or 'fecklessness' of poor people (rather than as a result of economic policies, structures and systems that reinforce inequality of income and wealth (Dorling, 2015)) serves to keep the wheels of power turning in such a way that wealth remains mainly in the hands of the few, rather than being more fairly distributed across the general population.

- **Discrimination**. This is one area where power is very much to the fore. Again, what we see is the pattern of dominance-subordination. Subordinate groups or categories of people come to be regarded as inferior or as a threat or both. This enables them to be subject to discrimination – that is to be treated in a less favourable way than other groups. Power is therefore at the heart of discrimination.

One of the implications of power being central to abuse (and therefore trauma) is that we have to be very careful how we use our own power (as adults and as professionals). Power generally operates 'below the surface' of society and so we can easily fail to recognise its workings. This means that if we are not 'power sensitive' we can easily reinforce relations of dominance and subordination, possibly at the expense of the children we are seeking to help on their journey of recovery.

> ### Key point
>
> Power relations are part and parcel of everyday life. They are not necessarily a bad thing in their own right (consider, for example, the use of legal powers to protect vulnerable people). However, when they are abused or misused, they can cause major problems and ruin people's lives. Power is also strongly implicated in sexual abuse and trauma, and so if we are not to add to the problems involved, we need to be sensitive to how power operates and be prepared to address the concerns that abuse or misuse raises.

Figure 7.2: Equality, diversity, inclusion and discrimination

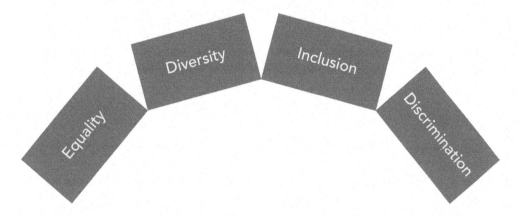

Ageism

We have already emphasised the significance of discrimination in society in general and in the lives of traumatised children. One aspect of this we need to take account of is the role of ageism. To begin with, ageism was seen as discrimination against older people. However, from these beginnings it evolved into an understanding of discrimination on the grounds of age more broadly, including discrimination against children and young people (Thompson, 2005).

There are various ways in which children can be discriminated against – for example, by being excluded from certain events or processes. At the time of a family bereavement in some cultures, children can be excluded from funerals, discussions of the bereaved or other aspects of grieving. This can then make it harder for them to deal with their feelings of distress (by missing out on the healing rituals involved) and leaves them less well-equipped to deal with losses in later life, having had no experience of funerals.

Age becomes a 'social marker' – that is, a feature of a person, group or category of people that can serve as the basis of discrimination. There can then be a two-way interaction, in the sense that age-related discrimination can add to the distress and challenging circumstances faced by traumatised children, while the impact of trauma can leave children less well equipped to deal with the challenges presented by ageism.

An important concept here is 'intersectionality' (May, 2015), which refers to how different forms of discrimination do not operate in isolation – they interact and create complex realities for the people concerned. For example, a black woman would not experience racism and sexism separately, but as intertwined dimensions of her experience. If she is also disabled, that that element will add further to the mix. It is therefore important to recognise that traumatised children's experiences of ageism will not arise in isolation; they will be part of a complex set of interactions involving other forms of discrimination.

Key point

Children are just as prone to discrimination as adults, if not more so because of ageism. If we disregard the significance of discrimination in children's lives, we will be neglecting a key aspect of their experience and thus render them less well equipped to take forward their journey of recovery from trauma.

Conclusion

This chapter began by acknowledging that the theory base underpinning childhood trauma has traditionally been individualistic in its focus. However there are important wider factors – cultural and structural – that can, and generally do, have a significant impact on the lives of traumatised children. If we are to do justice to the complex situations children have to wrestle with as part of their recovery, then we need to take account of the wider social factors, as well as the specific unique circumstances of each individual child – that is, we need to adopt a *psychosocial* understanding as part of our holistic approach that also includes biological and spiritual factors.

Unfortunately, as we have noted, there is a sad legacy of members of the caring professions either paying no attention to discrimination and oppression (taking no account of the impact of poverty, for example) or handling the complex issues involved in a simplistic and superficial way. It is therefore essential, if we are to achieve best practice, to make sure that we avoid these two unhelpful extremes; that we neither disregard the impact of wider social factors, nor handle them in ways that do not take into consideration how complex and sensitive they are.

Practice focus 7.3

Beverley was 11 when she came to live with us. She was a child of mixed heritage and had been sexually abused by her father. She had had multiple foster placements since she came into care, but they all broke down because of her difficult behaviour and she was labelled as 'unfosterable'. In one of her foster homes her foster mother found her scrubbing her skin with bleach. She told her therapist she hated being black because it meant she would be abused and if she was white she would be safe.

One effect of the oversimplification that took place was a considerable degree of anxiety and defensiveness and, with them, a tendency to try and avoid dealing with discrimination issues where possible, or to deal with them in tokenistic ways. Thankfully, that defensiveness has largely dissipated, but it would be both naïve and inaccurate to assume that it has gone away altogether. Examples of it are now far less frequent than was once the case, but they are still to be seen to this day. We therefore need to be careful not to allow any such defensiveness to creep into our practice.

A key issue in this regard is humility. Given that these are such complex and sensitive matters, we have to acknowledge that we will get it wrong sometimes, that discriminatory elements within our culture will emerge from time to time. However, what we need to do then is learn from the experience, rather than allow it to fuel an overcautious or defensive response. The children we serve need us to recognise our limitations (hence the term, humility), but to respond to them positively in a spirit of learning, rather than allow them to disempower us through an anxious defensiveness. Disempowering ourselves is not a helpful part of empowering traumatised children.

Points to ponder

1. Why might it be dangerous to think of equality as meaning sameness?

2. How might alienation hamper recovery?

3. What problems might arise if we disregard the significance of power in situations involving abuse and trauma?

Exercise

How would you describe your own ethnic or cultural background? What assumptions do you bring with you because of that background about:

■ children and their place in society

■ abuse and its impact

■ perpetrators of abuse

■ how best to help children

■ how to relate to people from a different cultural or ethnic background.

Chapter 8: Caring for the carers

Introduction

We have already emphasised the importance of making sure that the staff and foster carers who are working with abused and traumatised children receive appropriate support. In this chapter we explore these issues in a little bit more depth.

At the heart of caring for the carers is the idea of valuing people who are doing a very demanding job. It has been established for quite some time now that a demanding job is not necessarily a problematic job, provided that appropriate supports are put in place, and key among these is people feeling valued for what they do (Thompson, 2013).

It is vitally important that anyone working with traumatised children and young people is provided with appropriate support, because working with uncertainty is known to be something that can be potentially quite stressful (Barton *et al*, 2012) and of course working with traumatised children brings with it considerable uncertainty since there are no standard patterns of how children will respond to the difficult circumstances they find themselves in. This is important in terms of safeguarding the interests of both the children and their caregivers.

There is also the broader picture to consider, in the sense that organisations are likely to achieve better results if their employees have higher levels of personal well-being. For example, Robertson and Tinline (2008) argue that organisational cultures that support staff in developing high levels of well-being are likely to be the most effective ones in achieving their organisational goals.

The Mary Walsh Approach captures this idea perfectly, in so far as it was fully recognised that the most valuable part of the model is the staff group. If the staff are not looked after, and if they are not given the skills to do the job, if they are not given the knowledge and understanding to do the job, it is likely to be the children that suffer most, as they are deprived of the expert help they need on their journey of recovery. A key part of the approach has therefore been the recognition that the staff feel looked after and are given the tools to do the job properly. This involves not only good managerial working practices in terms of people management and workplace well-being (Thompson, 2013), but also the emotional containment or 'holding' that we discussed earlier.

The supporting of staff can be understood in relation to various aspects of organisational life, and it is worth exploring in more detail some of these main features.

Recruitment and selection

For all organisations, answering the question of how you know you are getting the right people is a vitally important one. Making mistakes at the recruitment and selection stage can have very problematic consequences further down the line. However, this is especially the case in recruiting staff to work with children who are experiencing the negative effects of abuse and trauma. It is therefore essential that proper attention is given to such matters, and that they are very carefully thought through. For example, it is important that appropriate police checks are made to ensure that actual or potential abusers are not allowed access to vulnerable children.

What is also important is ensuring that applicants appreciate what is involved in working with abused and traumatised children. The work is, by its very nature, very demanding (and therefore can be very rewarding), but if applicants have a rosy and unrealistic picture of what it is like to look after 'those poor, abused children', they are likely to have quite a shock when exposed to the harsh and demanding reality. Organisations should not go to the opposite extreme either, and have a sort of shock tactics approach, as that could well alienate potentially good applicants. Finding the middle line of realism is therefore an important factor. In this context, realism means being neither romantic and idealistic on the one hand, nor painting too dramatic and negative a picture on the other.

Key point

Working with traumatised children is richly rewarding work, but it is also very tough and challenging. Recruiting staff who are not able to respond positively to the challenges involved can be very harmful for the children and for the employees themselves (and for the reputation of the organisation as a whole). Getting recruitment right is therefore essential. Organisations that skimp on this aspect of human resources practice are taking major unnecessary risks.

In a similar vein, in terms of the recruitment and selection of foster carers, it is essential that a proper assessment is undertaken and that all applicants are made aware, through the process of assessment and associated training, of what impact having a traumatised child in their family home is likely to have on them, so that their readiness for such an event can be assessed and enhanced. In this way they can be helped to gain a clear picture of what is required of them.

For those working with traumatised children as an employee there is at least a chance of respite from the pressures of the job when not on duty and away from the workplace. However, for foster carers, these pressures are brought into their homes, and there may be few if any opportunities for respite from the pressures for them. We should therefore not underestimate how demanding being a foster carer is and always make sure that their efforts are valued and appreciated.

Workplace well-being

In recent years we have seen a growth of literature and attention around the subject of workplace well-being (Kinder *et al*, 2008; Robertson & Cooper, 2011; Schnall *et al*, 2009; Thompson & Bates, 2009). It has arisen partly in recognition of the fact that the modern workplace is potentially a stressful environment in which to work. However, it is important to recognise that stress is not inevitable if appropriate safeguards are put in place. The Health and Safety Executive define stress as what is experienced when our ability to cope with pressures is exceeded by the actual pressures[2] . That is, harmful stress arises not from the pressures themselves, but from situations where we feel unable to cope with those pressures.

Figure 8.1: Pressure and stress

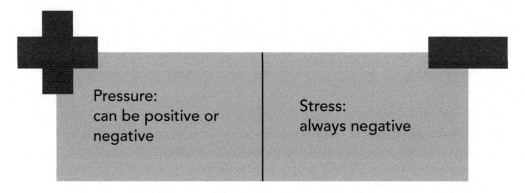

Pressure:
can be positive or negative

Stress:
always negative

---

2   http://www.hse.gov.uk/stress/what-to-do.htm (accessed August 2019).

Interestingly, this mirrors what is happening in the process of recovery – helping children to cope with the pressures they experience, rather than trying to reach a Holy Grail situation of there being no pressures.

The term 'workplace well-being' encompasses the endeavours to make sure that pressures are kept at reasonable levels. It is based on the recognition that everybody benefits from this – staff, managers and the organisation itself, as there are far fewer problems this way. A manageable amount of pressure can be rewarding and enriching, stimulating and motivating, whereas once that level becomes excessive it can do a great deal of harm to the health and well-being of the carers involved.

This can be understood to apply in terms of two sets of issues. First of all, it is important that staff providing care have reasonable expectations of what they can achieve, and this will come from two directions:

1. It will need to come from the organisation itself: is the organisation placing unrealistic expectations on staff or foster carers, or are they being suitably realistic in terms of what can be achieved with current levels of staffing resources?

2. There is the set of expectations deriving from the carers themselves. Here, an important concept once again is that of 'humility', by which we mean the recognition that we cannot have a completely successful approach to working with traumatised children. A 100% success rate is not possible, of course, however much we would like it to be. It is unfortunately the case that members of the caring professions often make the mistake of feeling guilty if they do not achieve it. In reality, of course, this is highly problematic, because it means that people are creating obstacles to their own job satisfaction and they block their own ability to attain a sense of achievement. That humility (the recognition that we can only do our best in difficult circumstances and cannot expect success at all times) can be an important way of fending off stress. It 'keeps us real' by not allowing us to give ourselves unrealistic expectations that can: (a) be an unnecessary source of pressure in their own right; and (b) sap our confidence by giving us a strong sense that we are doomed to fail.

The second important set of issues in terms of avoiding stress is being prepared for the emotional demands involved in the work. This brings us back to the important concept of emotional holding and also introduces the concept of 'emotional competence'. We will return to this theme below, as it is worthy of detailed exploration in its own right.

Key point

In everyday language, the terms 'pressure' and 'stress' are often used interchangeably. However, from a technical point of view they are different. Pressure can be positive or negative, depending on the circumstances, but stress is always negative – a source of harm – because it refers to what arises when we are not able to cope with the pressures we face. We should therefore be careful not to confuse pressure and stress, and we should appreciate the differences.

An appropriate level of training and development will also help reduce the effects of stress. We believe that this needs to cover two interlinking sets of issues. On the one hand, it is important that carers are helped to develop a theory base that will make sense to them in practice. Having an understanding of theory simply for its own sake is of little use, but we should also recognise that focusing on practice without an adequate underlying theory base that will help to make sense of the complexities involved is potentially very dangerous. Our first concern, therefore, in terms of training and development is that there should be an integration of theory and practice as a fundamental part of reflective practice.

This brings us back to the work of Thompson (2017a) we touched on in Chapter 3, in which we discussed the idea of theorising practice, which involves beginning with practice and using theory (our professional knowledge base) to make sense of it, rather than the more traditional approach of starting with theory and trying to 'apply' it to practice. It is important that people working with traumatised children therefore have at least a basic understanding of key issues such as the nature and consequences of trauma, the role of attachment, the significance of power dynamics, and so on. The fuller that knowledge base the better, as this will mean that carers are not only better equipped to provide well-informed support, but will also be more confident in their practice because of their higher level of understanding.

Second, it is important that there is an important linkage between head and heart. That is, while rational theoretical issues drawn from research and social science concepts can be very helpful, they also need to be complemented by an understanding of the emotional side of working with children, both the emotions that the children will be displaying themselves and, of course, the emotions of the carers themselves. Training and development are therefore issues that need to be given considered attention, rather than seen as a matter of providing basic training courses in a routine or mechanistic way (that is, there needs to be a *professional* approach to training and development, rather than a bureaucratic one).

> ## Practice focus 8.1
>
> Sexual abuse is a syndrome of secrecy and denial and it is compelling for people caring for these children to engage in denial of the severity of the abuse – for example, 'they're just being naughty', and in keeping secrets with the children particularly about their stories. In consultancy and training the staff were helped to see that it was really important to be open minded and to understand the meaning behind the behaviours, and to refuse to keep secrets. They were also helped to see the difference between secrets and surprises. Surprises can be wonderful, but secrets must not be entered into.

Training and development also need to be complemented by high-quality supervision. Thompson and Gilbert (2019) make the important point that supervision should not simply be a matter of focusing on individual cases as part of a bureaucratic process of checking up. It should focus on reviewing how the carer is operating in terms of their knowledge, skills and values and their own emotional responses to what are likely to be very challenging situations. How supervision is conceptualised varies from profession to profession and organisation to organisation, but we should not allow this diversity to lead us to lose sight of its fundamental basis, which is to provide 'supervision' literally – that is, an overview which will be supportive to the member of staff or carer concerned. Supervision should help each carer to do the best they can and to grow and develop in the process.

> ## Key point
>
> In some organisations, supervision becomes reduced to a simple process of case management (and can easily be reduced further to a matter of checking up on staff). This is a great pity, as the staff support, staff development and conflict management aspects of supervision have an extremely important part to play in helping staff to be the best they possibly can.

All these factors (stress avoidance, training and development, and supervision) need to be part of and supported by a supportive and safe organisational culture. An organisational culture is a set of habits, unwritten rules and taken-for-granted assumptions that can be very powerful influences on how people behave, how they think and how they react emotionally to their workplace encounters. Leadership is now recognised as an important factor in shaping organisational culture in a positive direction (Gilbert, 2005; Thompson, 2016a). We will therefore return to the key issue of leadership below.

Emotional competence

The notion of emotional intelligence has become a highly popular one and has often been oversimplified. There is some doubt as to whether intelligence is the appropriate term (Fineman, 2000), and so we are using what we see as a preferable term: 'emotional competence'. The basic idea is that, with practice, we can exercise a degree of control over our emotional responses and we can also learn how to read effectively the non-verbal signals that are giving us clues about other people's emotional states. It is not a case of trying to be 'rational' or 'objective' and thereby attempting to suppress our feelings. Rather, it is more a matter of balancing head and heart and thereby doing fuller justice to the complexities of being human. Trying to focus on rationality (head) alone means that we are neglecting a significant part of the human experience, while letting our emotions run free (heart) can be counterproductive, and even dangerous at times. Trying to suppress or stifle emotions (that is, going beyond trying to balance them with rationality) can also be counterproductive. For example, trying to suppress anger without actually dealing with it sensibly and sensitively (balancing head and heart) can mean that it re-emerges as depression.

Emotional competence is essential because of the emotional intensity of the work involved. Therefore, what is crucial for effective practice in working towards trauma recovery is the ability to 'stay with it', to be robust in working our way through some very difficult circumstances and some very challenging encounters. It also involves 'thinking the unthinkable' – being able to recognise the horrific nature of abuse and the devastating effects of trauma but still remain strong enough and positive enough to guide the children on their journey towards recovery.

Cairns helps us to understand the importance of supporting adults involved in this difficult and demanding work of promoting recovery in traumatised children:

'It is particularly important to recognise that living with traumatised children evokes strong feelings and powerful dynamics. Every family is at risk of becoming dangerously disordered when living with such disorder. It is vital that good supervision and support are available to families providing therapeutic parenting. Such supervision should be emotionally responsive enough to carry the family through the many turbulent experiences that will assail them, and professionally informed enough to be able to discern the points at which the family is slipping towards the powerful vortex of disorder that follows traumatic stress.'
(2002, pii)

The important message of this passage can, of course, be extended to relate to anyone who works in the emotionally highly charged world of traumatised children.

It cannot be emphasised enough, then, that people working with children traumatised by abuse need to have a high degree of emotional competence. Such work is of a highly emotive nature that often involves dealing with raw emotions (grief, sorrow, bitterness, anger, rage, disappointment, fear, aggression, guilt, shame, despair and any confused and confusing mixture of them). It is therefore essential that carers have a reasonable degree of self-awareness that will put them in a stronger position to respond to the challenges involved. Indeed, self-awareness is a key component of emotional competence, as it involves being tuned in to our own feelings and the effects they are having on us – this is part of the idea of finding a balance of head and heart.

Key point

The traditional emphasis in education and training is on 'head' (thinking and cognitive matters), but there are many forms of work – especially working with traumatised children – where 'heart' (emotional or 'affective' matters) are also of major significance and need to be included in our learning and development efforts.

A key issue here is the distinction between sympathy and empathy. Sympathy refers to sharing the same feelings as the person or persons we are engaged with. If, for example, we are working with somebody who is disappointed, then sympathy would mean that we are disappointed too. If they are anxious, then we are anxious too, and so on. Empathy, by contrast, is where we are able to recognise and respond appropriately to another person's emotions, but we do not necessarily share those emotions at that time.

Clearly what is required of us in working with traumatised children is empathy, rather than sympathy, in so far as we would not be able to last very long in terms of our own stresses and strains if we were constantly sharing the feelings that abused children are having. However, at the other extreme, if we went from sympathy to apathy and did not engage with the feelings dimension at all, we would be practising in a highly dangerous way. The balancing point between sympathy and apathy, then, is empathy, and that is what we need to be encouraging and supporting in the emotional responses of carers.

Figure 8.2: Sympathy, empathy and apathy

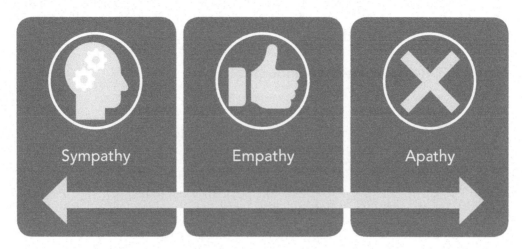

Key to this is the idea of 'holding', as discussed earlier. Organisations need to create an atmosphere where staff feel held. Mary recognises the significance of this in her work and has put a great deal of emphasis on the need to provide the sort of emotionally supportive environment that is essential for best practice. This is not necessarily an easy matter, as staff have emotional challenges of their own to deal with, especially in such a demanding line of work. It can often take more energy to create a safe environment for the staff than for the children, so the effort required should not be underestimated. This links well with the challenges of leadership, another important topic we shall explore below.

Mary has also acknowledged the difficulties involved, recognising that it took quite some time to get matters right when it comes to 'caring for the carers'. She acknowledges that it was a learning curve for her, for her senior team, and indeed for the staff themselves. The journey involved learning how to best nurture staff so that they can give the best service to the children and thus to their employers.

Nurturing is very much the appropriate word, as it does not mean wrapping people up in cotton wool or patronising them in any way, but it does mean being fully supportive in recognition of the immense challenges – personal and professional – in undertaking this important work.

Nurturing is a key part of holding. What also needs to be involved in a holding environment is what Papadatou (2009) refers to as being 'vulnerable enough'. She advocates the need for a balance between being too vulnerable (and thereby allowing circumstances to overwhelm us) and not being vulnerable enough, which means that we are seeing ourselves as invulnerable and not open to the emotional challenges involved in the work. There is a parallel here, of course, with the idea of empathy, and so a balance of vulnerability – not too much, not too little – fits well with the idea of empathy.

Figure 8.3: Being 'vulnerable enough'

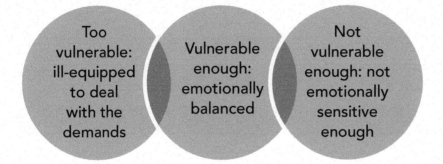

One very relevant consideration here is that of gender. The literature relating to the sociology of emotions has long recognised that there are differences in how men and women tend to deal with emotions, and strong gender-related patterns of emotional response (Fischer, 2000). Organisations need to be aware of this and tuned in to the subtleties of what is involved. This is because there are two dangerous extremes to avoid: one is to ignore gender altogether and just treat staff and foster carers as individuals (thereby potentially missing some very significant gender-related aspects of their emotional response, as we noted in Chapter 7). The other is to rely on gender stereotypes (for example, to assume that women are more emotional than men). A healthy balance between these two unhelpful extremes would recognise the complexities involved and be sensitive to the fact that, as discussed earlier, we are all unique individuals, but unique individuals in a social context – and gender is a key factor when it comes to understanding the social context.

One of the reasons this is important is that it has to be recognised that everyone will have their own 'baggage', in the sense that none of us will be able to approach situations without our own emotional issues to deal with. That is, of course, part and parcel of being human, and so we cannot expect people to come to emotionally demanding work with a clean slate, as it were, with no emotional issues of their own to wrestle with. Holding therefore needs to include creating and protecting a space for carers' own issues to be addressed. This does not mean that we expect supervisors to be counsellors or therapists to their staff, but there should be at least a basic recognition that the work being undertaken will have emotional consequences, and that organisations that fail to address these issues can be dangerous places for the health and well-being of the staff, and therefore for the safety, development and well-being of the children.

Another important concept is the notion of secondary or vicarious trauma (Quitangon, 2015). This refers to the idea that people who are engaged in supporting or working with people who have been traumatised can become traumatised themselves. This is a phenomenon that is well documented in relation to disaster work (see, for example, Raphael, 1990). However, it would be foolish not to be alert to the fact that it can also apply to working with children, and so organisations need to have an awareness at all levels of the dangers of vicarious trauma and put in place systems for ensuring that carers are adequately supported against this arising.

Key point

Ironically, working with traumatised children can be a source of trauma for the carers. Such 'vicarious' trauma is sadly quite common in some settings, and so it is essential the staff care and support issues are taken seriously. Both the staff and the children will lose out, potentially in major ways, if not.

A further important concept is that of compassion fatigue. This term is used in two senses. On the one hand, it can refer to the way in which the media are constantly giving accounts of dreadful occurrences around the world (wars, terrorism, natural disasters, and so on) that can make it very easy for readers of the newspaper or consumers of other media to reach a point of compassion fatigue, whereby the pains and suffering simply wash over them (Moeller, 1999) – they become insensitive to the pain and suffering that are reported, and often visually represented, on our screens and in our publications, or by other means. This is an important issue in its own right, but it also relates specifically to working with traumatised children, in so far as there is a danger that their pain and suffering can become 'normalised' to busy, pressurised staff, who may become insensitive to their plight if compassion fatigue is allowed to set in.

However, what is perhaps equally pertinent in relation to working with traumatised children is the idea of compassion fatigue in relation to what has come to be known as emotional labour (Hochschild, 1983). This refers to situations where people need to draw on their own emotional resources as part of their work. It is a form of enforced emotionality that can range from relatively straightforward matters, such as sales assistants being called upon to smile and look cheerful, even when they are feeling far from happy, to the far more challenging demands of working towards trauma recovery. These much more telling experiences of emotional labour involve having to work with children who may be brimming over with intense negative emotions that can be exhausting and, indeed, potentially traumatising in their own right over time.

Organisations therefore need to be aware of the potential for compassion fatigue – for example by putting it explicitly on the agenda and giving opportunities through appropriate fora to discuss emotional matters. This takes us back to the notion of organisational culture. The Waterhouse Report (Waterhouse, 2000) cautioned against environments where children are looked after that come to be characterised by a 'macho' approach (another gender issue). This sort of hypermasculine stoicism has no place in the care of traumatised children. It is vitally important that the intense emotional nature of the work is acknowledged and dealt with openly and constructively, without any attempt to try and brush those feelings under the carpet.

Barton *et al* (2012) argue that working with traumatised children presents potential concerns in terms of boundaries and the anxieties that can be generated from a lack of clarity about boundaries. They argue that:

'In reality, organisations that work with traumatised children can expect considerable difficulty in maintaining effective boundary management. There are a number of reasons for this. The work involves significant levels of anxiety that will impact on those directly working with children and the whole organisation. Maintaining clear boundaries is particularly difficult when people are anxious and where boundaries are being continually tested.'
(2012, p129)

This has important implications for how staff are supported, and again reinforces the need for issues to be discussed openly without any culture of stoic avoidance.

Overall, then, it can be seen that the type of work we have been describing in this book is potentially emotionally damaging for all concerned, and so important safeguards must be put in place to promote an appropriate level of emotional competence – partly for health and safety reasons to ensure that staff and foster carers are not exposed to undue levels of psychological harm, and partly for child care reasons in terms of making sure that children get the best level of support possible. This is quite a challenging undertaking, but there are two plus points to the situation. On the one hand, it means that we are better placed to provide a positive and helpful recovery experience for children whose lives have been devastated by abuse. On the other hand, it can also be incredibly enriching for staff to develop their emotional competence, as these skills, and the confidence that comes with them, can be exceptionally helpful in dealing with all aspects of their life, both within and outside the workplace.

Rising to these significant challenges can be helped by high-quality leadership, while poor or non-existent leadership can add to what are already significant difficulties.

Leadership

The point was made earlier that leadership involves having a positive influence on the organisational culture. This means that leaders are expected to have the skills to influence their staff ('followers') in a positive direction by challenging problematic aspects of a culture (a tendency for staff to form cliques that exclude certain colleagues, for example) and reinforcing the positive, helpful ones (a strong commitment to learning and continuous professional development, for example). This is extremely important, as leadership can make the difference between an effective and an ineffective organisation, and so for organisations that work with traumatised children, leadership can make the difference as to whether the child is helped to recover or not; whether they are plagued by the harmful experiences they have encountered or are able to move forward and establish a much-better quality of life. Kelloway *et al* refer to research that supports the idea that leadership can have a very positive impact on well-being in the workplace:

'The suggestion that leaders have an impact on employees' well-being is neither novel nor particularly startling. Research documenting the effects of leadership on employee well-being has been available for over 30 years (Day & Hamblin, 1964) and the conclusions of this research would not surprise any adult who has held a job for any length of time (Gilbreath, 2004). Poor leadership is associated with increased levels of employee stress (Offerman & Hellman, 1996; Richman et al, 1992) alienation (Ashforth, 1994; 1997) and may provoke counter-productive behaviors such as retaliation (Townsend et al, 2000). What may be surprising is just how extensive are the effects of leadership on individuals' well-being.' (2008, p25)

These comments reinforce the significance of having good-quality leadership to guide people through the difficult, often stormy waters of working in the field of trauma recovery.

Leadership is also important in terms of developing a culture of reflective practice. Thompson explains reflective practice in the following terms:

'Reflective practice provides fertile soil for learning in a number of ways, not least the following:

■ *It involves drawing on theory, research and the professional knowledge base more broadly and therefore provides a constant stream of opportunities to gain new insights from that knowledge base.*

■ *It encourages us to be creative, to move beyond formula solutions and look at a range of possible ways forward. This allows us to have a fresh and open approach to each new situation we encounter and thus be open to new ideas.*

■ *It entails reflection-on-action, looking back over a piece of work in order to learn from it – evaluating our practice, not necessarily in a formal sense, but none the less in ways that enable us to benefit from the lessons of experience.*

■ *It recognises the complexity and variability of the problems and situations ... workers encounter and therefore helps to sensitise us to the rich diversity of the social world and the need to remain alert to its subtleties and intricacies. That is, it discourages us from oversimplifying the challenges we face.'*

(2002, p107)

It is important that such practice is embedded within the organisational culture and is not just seen as something that some people will do and others will not. Ideally, for optimal levels of performance, it has to be seen as an essential component of good practice and not as an optional extra. Carers will encounter very complex situations and, if they are not engaging with these in a reflective, mindful way, there is a danger that they will respond inappropriately and potentially make the situation worse.

A key aspect of leadership is the idea of creating new leaders. As long ago as 1923, Mary Parker Follett wrote about the importance of leadership being empowering. Leadership, she argued, is not to be defined by the exercise of power but by the capacity to increase the sense of power among those who are being led. The task of a leader, therefore, is to create leaders. This is an important concept, as it reinforces the idea that carers need to engage in a reflective way with their practice, that they have to be, in a sense, leaders in their own right.

It is also important to return to the theme of spirituality. This is because a key part of spirituality is the idea of having a sense of purpose and direction which, of course, is also a feature of leadership. A good leader can create an atmosphere in which people have a sense of purpose and are motivated by that. They can also have a sense of connectedness, and a sense that they are part of something bigger than themselves in terms of having a value commitment to making a positive difference to the lives of children who have had dreadful experiences of abuse. This, then, is another example of the importance of having a spiritual dimension to our work (Moss, 2009).

Both spirituality and leadership are issues (or sets of issues) that the Mary Walsh Approach has taken seriously since its early days. An important part of leadership that chimes well with the spiritual notion of having a sense of purpose and direction is that of vision. An effective leader is someone who is able to engage people in shaping the vision and in achieving it together. This has long been a feature of Mary's philosophy. The vision of the company was to be the driving force to ensure that traumatised children will have the right to recover from their injuries, and this 'right' has played a central role. We give children who have been physically hurt the right, the immediate right, to treatment, so we would be outraged if a child had a broken leg and did not go immediately to hospital and have it set. But for children who have got emotional injuries, the same right is not recognised or respected, and yet the consequences of emotional injury and trauma are likely to be far greater than a broken leg, for example.

Finally, in terms of leadership, it can be seen as a key requirement that leaders are able to instil a sense of confidence and nurture a degree of courage in the people they lead. Working with traumatised children, as we have emphasised, is immensely demanding work, but it can also be immensely rewarding if we make the commitment to making it work. This brings huge challenges and can be physically, intellectually and emotionally draining at times. However, having the confidence and the commitment to go on, to work through the difficulties because of the crucially important nature of this type of work, can be an incredible asset. Effective leadership is not enough on its own to bring about this commitment, but it certainly has a central role to play within it.

Key point

Leadership should not be seen as purely the domain of managers. All professionals can be seen to have a responsibility for making a contribution to developing and sustaining a positive culture. It is shared responsibility for the common benefit of all who work in the organisation and, of course, the children it serves.

Conclusion

Caring for the carers is clearly of central importance in working with traumatised children. If we are not able to protect staff and foster carers from the damaging consequences of intense emotionality and the stresses and strains that trauma-related work brings, then they will not be in a good position to offer the care and support that the children need. To make sure that the children are receiving the best help they can, we have to make sure that carers are functioning at optimal levels which in turn means that we have to take very seriously indeed the notions of workplace well-being, of training and development, supervision, emotional competence and, of course, leadership. It is to be hoped that this chapter has helped to provide a platform of understanding that will enable practitioners and managers to work towards improving the level of support that staff and foster carers receive.

Children who are abused often suffer at the hands of parents whose own needs have not been met. It is therefore vitally important that we do not allow the possibility of carers' needs not being met to get in the way of their doing the best job possible. Getting it right in terms of staff and carer support is therefore an essential requirement, not an optional extra. It is to be hoped that the discussions in this chapter will help to cast some light on how that can be done.

Conclusion

This book began with a set of discussions describing a set of journeys that have come together in significant ways. Mary's own part in this story was of course crucial in the shaping of the development of her approach, and underpinning all this was the major influence of the journey of ideas – the key theoretical and philosophical ideas that have underpinned the Mary Walsh Approach and subsequently the wide range of people who have been influenced by it. The organisation Mary co-founded was in existence for over 25 years and, during that time, not only helped thousands of children during that time on their journey towards recovery, but also helped to embed her ideas in the work of very many practitioners far and wide; across the world in fact.

Much was learned during those years and no doubt much learning will continue to occur. This book has been produced as, in some ways, a testimony to the learning that has taken place so far and, we hope it will play a part in fostering further learning in the years to come.

The journey towards recovery is, as we have seen, generally a difficult and demanding one, but it is none the less a vitally important one. As Johnston *et al* help us to understand, it is about helping victimised children to escape from the prison of their trauma, so that they can lead full and fulfilling lives without their health and well-being being adversely affected by earlier experiences of abuse. They describe how traumatised children develop unhelpful patterns of responding to their life experiences:

'Without intervention, these patterns (or scripts) form a prism that allows in signals of interpersonal threat while filtering out more benign information. As a result, the child feels, paradoxically, both confirmed in his or her view of the interpersonal world as dangerous and yet safe, because he or she can scan for and control the threat. As these patterns consolidate, they mitigate against the child's capacity to trust others and to tolerate intimacy with others. The prism therefore becomes a prison as children's opportunities for cognitive and emotional growth are limited to the confines of the script. The result, to varying degrees, is emotional constriction, avoidance of feelings and genuine interpersonal contact, difficulty experiencing empathy with others, and distortions in moral reasoning and conduct.'
(2009, p57)

Upon Mary's retirement in 2013, the organisation she co-founded ceased to exist as an independent entity, as it was taken over by a larger child care organisation that introduced its own approach to the children served These changes have not diminished the impact and the current practice of her model in organisations across the world. As an example, the assessment framework has proved to be the foundation of child recovery assessments undertaken in Australia (Berry Street and Lighthouse – see Tomlinson *et al* (2012); Rose (2012)). Many of the senior employees who have been trained and then entrusted in managing the Walsh Recovery System have current roles in leading child trauma organisations. Nine of the most senior people from Mary's team have current director positions, which have allowed her model to continue to influence the recovery of children and young people across the country and beyond.

Mary has reflected on her professional journey over the last 30-plus years. The development of this book and the discussions that led up to it have allowed for acknowledgement of her belief that children can recover to a greater or lesser extent from the most awful of starts in life. The determination of her team in providing a service centred on the child, and not on those adults around the child, has successfully assisted children to lead healthy lives in their adulthood. It is not a magic solution, it is a tried and trusted method of helping children that is far superior to the traditional idea of simply hoping that children removed to a loving place of safety will, in time, 'get over it'. In the first years of the work of Mary and her team, they were campaigning for adults to listen to what children were saying, not just through their spoken word, but their whole presentation – thinking of the child holistically. From badges stating that the wearer 'listens to children' to training materials and keynote presentations at national conferences, this fundamental requirement that her staff listen to, believe and take seriously the children they engage with has been central to practice. Scandals in the UK that have come to light since 2013 have demonstrated the importance of listening to the unbelievable, to the essential notion of taking children and what they say seriously – even after these high profile cases (Jimmy Saville, Rolf Harris and others, and no doubt many others yet to come to light), denial remains rife as we, as a society, seem to find it hard to accept that such things occur.

Sadly, many of our most vulnerable children are at risk and failed by the system that still finds it hard to take children and their stories as true. While there will be occasional cases on record of children who have made false allegations, it has to be recognised that these form a very tiny proportion of situations where disclosures are made. Our first and major reaction must be to listen to what the child has to say and take their concerns seriously.

Mary continues to make a contribution through her work with IRCT (the Institute for Recovery from Childhood Trauma) and the training and consultancy that she and her colleagues provide across the country and beyond. However, she recognises that there is still much to be done, not only with the children who will, sadly, continue to need the help the service offers, but also in educating others and seeking to influence policy in relation to children's services and the lack of investment in trauma recovery. In this regard, Bradshaw makes an important point in arguing that:

'The true measure of a nation's standing is how well it attends to its children – their health and safety, their material safety, their education and socialization, and their sense of being loved, valued, and included in the families and societies into which they were born (UNICEF, 2007, p 1)'
(2011, p1)

To this we could perhaps add that how well it responds to the recovery needs of children traumatised by abuse is also a measure of a nation's standing, of how committed to the well-being of its citizens it is, especially its junior citizens and those among them who have suffered the ordeal of being abused by people they should have been able to trust. In the UK there is a clear approach for children and young people who have been or who are likely to be sexually exploited and trafficked by unscrupulous people from all cultures within our city centres and within our rural communities. Over the last 30-plus years of practising in protective services for children and trauma recovery, Mary is aware of several events that draw the attention of the public and then attract the media, and finally the government to respond – whether we consider episodes like Cleveland, Ricky Neave, Victoria Climbié, Baby Peter or the Rochdale and Rotherham sex scandals – each became front page news, grabbed the imagination of the nation and became in its own way 'sexy'. This phenomenon leads to valuable and scarce resources being diverted to these high-level, publicity-rich cases and away from the children who are being abused day in day out within their own families, shrouded in secrecy and denial, diminishing their rights to be protected and given the care they need. When this happens, these children are invisible, not heard and, unless there are compelling reasons not to, the support structure that the children need is withdrawn. It is not surprising to hear that at least 1,400 children in one local authority were abused over a period of years, traumatised by significant adults in their lives and not heard by those whose job is was to protect them – these children grow up with a notion of hurt, a history of pain and difficulties in engaging in society as healthy, capable adults[3].

---

3   https://en.wikipedia.org/wiki/Rochdale_child_sex_abuse_ring (accessed August 2019)

Children who are trafficked and abused in what should be caring environments have entered a horrific and life-changing world. Children who have experienced a poor early childhood might be more susceptible to exploitation, but this particular crime is party to peer pressure, seduction and attention – often these latter elements could be attractive to any young impressionable child. This is hard to engage with, but children who have been abused throughout their lives and have distorted thoughts and feelings as a result of what has happened to them are likely to have deep-seated internal working models, which may lead to difficulties in relationships, esteem and presentation. Mary and her team developed an approach that meets the needs of these children, where support and guidance is not enough. The Mary Walsh Approach is designed to deliver a sense of recovery for children by addressing their internal and external realities. In doing so, the children are able to create opportunities to understand and accept the events of their life and to move forward through their life, rather than being led by their past.

No one can rewind the clock and stop the harm from being done, but with skilled, well-informed intervention by committed staff and carers operating within a clear value base, there is much that can be done to empower traumatised children and young people so that they can move forward positively. This book has introduced a distinctive and well-tried approach to the process of recovery for children and engagement for those working with children. As we noted in Chapter 2, Mary and her team developed a clear value base that should be at the centre of any organisation working with children and seeking to assist them in achieving best outcomes.

Mary and her team have provided much-needed help for very many children and have assisted a wide range of other organisations throughout its many years of operation (through its training programme and publications, for example) to provide help for many more children. However, this important journey continues through the children who have benefited from its programme and for the staff who continue to work with children across the world. Mary continues her journey to promote and demand that all of us work towards providing the best of care to children who are traumatised by abuse and that we are all supported in assisting best practice. This should not be limited by the tools we currently have and the goodwill of the people who contribute on the front line; it should be a societal commitment that is not contained by what we can afford to do, or what we can do, but by what we must do.

As a society, we need to continue to invest heavily in safeguarding children from abuse and to make sure that those funds are used widely and not wasted on unnecessary (and demoralising) bureaucracy (Munro, 2011). However, there is also a very pressing need for further significant investment in recovery services to ensure, as far as possible, that the aftermath of abuse is not a story of ongoing fear, distress and emotional turmoil, but one of rebuilding, of constructing a new, empowering narrative of healing. As Rymaszewska and Philpot so aptly put it:

'... too many children who have been damaged by their experiences at the hands of others pass from an unsafe environment to a physically safe one without what should be the necessary bridge on that journey, a means of moving on from an abusive life to a satisfactory new one, from hurt to recovery.'
(2006, p14)

Mary Walsh and her team established important foundations to meet the needs of extremely traumatised children from the age of four to adulthood. The challenge continues to confront all of us in society, and we need to do much more to meet the needs of our vulnerable and hurt children and young people. We need to keep asking ourselves and those around us whether we are doing as much as we reasonably can to help children whose lives have been blighted by abuse and trauma to have a way out, to have the option of recovery, so that they can heal the wounds of their maltreatment and exploitation and develop a much safer, more satisfying and fulfilling life, and not have to live in fear or with a sense of shame or inadequacy.

We owe it to not only the current generation of children, but also to future generations to get this right, as there is a very real danger that a proportion of the children who are not afforded the opportunity to recover will go on to abuse others and begin the cycle all over again.

Prevention and therapeutic responses must always work hand in hand. As long as there are children in the world who are exposed to abuse and neglect, we have a duty to respond not just to the physical injury, but to the enormous and distorting emotional damage done to young minds.

Childhood is our learning place, where we learn how things are; we learn how things work, and we learn rules, values and culture – in short, we learn how to be. So a good childhood for children at Berry Street, for example, is achievable by replicating healthier early life experiences – providing care, love, boundaries, clues, commentary, engagement, stimulation, opportunities for success and support.

Our best work with hurt children is to be there when they fall, help them to get up, support them, guide them and role model positive outcomes. Traumatised children are not monsters; they have had monstrous things happen to them. Earlier in this book we spoke of sexual trauma as akin to physical trauma, and to this end we repeat Mary's long-held view that trauma of the body is not confined to a breakage, scar or visual impediment – trauma affects the body, the mind, the emotional core, the spirit and the future well-being of the child, hence our emphasis on a holistic approach. When a child breaks a leg, we comfort the child; we support their leg and wrap it with a structure that is strong, resilient, and encompassing. After a while, the structure is removed, and the child is provided with therapy until their leg is strong enough to function as it was intended. Children traumatised by abuse have not got the visual injuries similar to that of a broken leg; nonetheless they are as hurt, in as much pain, and often as immobilised by their injury. We need to provide them with comfort, with structure and ensure that this structure is strong, resilient and encompassing too. This provides the environment that permits the child to heal, to become strong and to reach a point where they have learned to operate in age-appropriate ways, to trust and to allow themselves to be loved, to be lovable and to be safe.

In the 25th year of Mary's tenure as the head of the organisation she co-founded, she presented all the adults who were charged with providing care to children and young people with a starfish specially commissioned to celebrate 25 years of making a difference to children, reflecting the importance of the starfish story we encountered in Chapter 1. This story was retold to help all those involved to understand that the enormity of the task ahead of them could be overwhelming, but that still did not mean that a difference for their child could not be achieved if they focused on that child.

In writing this book, we have been hoping that we are helping you to be able to see that we all have the ability to make a difference. And, if we can, like the starfish story helps us to do, remain aware of this and alert to its significance, we can help shape the future for the children we work with.

Sadly, there is no difficulty in finding starfish, there are thousands – the difficulty is how we ensure that each one is gently guided, despite the potential 'choppy waters', to safety.

References

Adams, K. (2009) 'The Rise of the Child's Voice; the Silencing of the Spiritual Voice', *Journal of Beliefs and Values*, **30**(2).

Alexander, J. C. (2012) *Trauma: A Social Theory*, Cambridge, Polity Press.

Archer, C. and Burnell, A. (eds) (2003) *Trauma, Attachment and Placement: Fear Can Stop You Loving*, London, Jessica Kingsley Publishers.

Ashforth, B. (1994) 'Petty Tyranny in Organizations', *Human Relation*, 47, pp. 755-778.

Ashforth, B. (1997) 'Petty Tyranny in Organizations: A Preliminary Examination of Antecedents and Consequences', *Canadian Journal of Administrative Sciences*, 14, pp. 1173-1182.

Attig, T. (2011) *How We Grieve: Relearning the World*, 2nd edn, New York, Oxford University Press.

Back, L. (2007) *The Art of Listening*, Oxford, Berg.

Barnes, V. (2018) *Child-Centred Social Work: Theory and Practice*, London, Palgrave.

Barry, B. (2005) *Why Social Justice Matters*, Cambridge, Polity Press.

Barton, S., Gonzalez, R. and Tomlinson, P. (2012) *Therapeutic Residential Care for Children and Young People: An Attachment and Trauma-Informed Model for Practice*, London, Jessica Kingsley.

Bates, J., Pugh, R. and Thompson, N. (eds) (1999) *Protecting Children: Challenges and Change*, Aldershot, Arena.

Bauman, Z. (1991) *Modernity and the Holocaust*, Cambridge, Polity.

Bell, S. (1988) *When Salem Came to the Boro: The True Story of the Cleveland Child Abuse Crisis*, London, Pan.

Bentall, R. P. (2010) *Doctoring the Mind: Why psychiatric treatments fail*. London: Penguin.

Bentovim, A. (2002) 'Preventing Sexually Abused Young People from Becoming Abusers, and Treating the Victimization Experiences of Young People who Offend Sexually', *Child Abuse and Neglect*, 26, pp. 661-678.

Barton, S. Gonzales, R. and Tomlinson, P. (2011) *Therapeutic Residential Care for Children and Young People*, London, Jessica Kingsley.

Bentovim, A., Cox, A., Miller, L. B. and Pizzey, S. (eds) (2009) *Safeguarding Children Living with Trauma and family Violence: Evidence-based Assessment, Analysis and Planning Interventions*, London, Jessica Kingsley.

Bion, W. R. (1962) *Learning from Experience*, London, Karnac.

Bowlby, J. (1969) *Attachment and Loss: Vol 1 Attachment*, London, Hogarth Press.

Bowlby, J. (1979) *The Making and Breaking of Affectional Bonds*, London, Tavistock.

Boylan, J. and Dalrymple, J. (2009) *Understanding Advocacy for Children and Young People*, Maidenhead, Open University Press.

Bracken, P. (2002) *Trauma: Culture, Meaning and Philosophy*, London, Whurr.

Bracken, P. and Thomas, P. (2005) *Postpsychiatry: Mental Health in a Postmodern World*, Oxford, Oxford University Press.

Bradshaw, J. (ed.) (2011) *The Well-being of Children in the UK*, 3rd edn, Bristol, The Policy Press.

Briere, J. N. (1992) *Child Abuse Trauma: Theory and Treatment of the Lasting Effects*, London, Sage.

Buber, M. (2013) *I-Thou*, London, Bloomsbury.

Cairns, K. (2002) *Attachment, Trauma and Resilience: Therapeutic Caring for Children*, London, BAAF.

Calhoun, L. G. and Tedeschi, R. G. (1999) *Facilitating Post-traumatic Growth: A Clinician's Guide*, New York, Routledge.

Campbell, B. (1988) *Unofficial Secrets: Child Abuse – The Cleveland Case*, London, Virago.

Canfield, J. and Hansen, M. V. (2000) *Chicken Soup for the Soul*, London, Vermilion.

Carroll, N. (1990) *The Philosophy of Horror: Or Paradoxes of the Heart*, London, Routledge.

Cooper, C. L. and Robertson, I. (eds) (2004) *International Review of Industrial and Organizational Psychology*, Volume 19.

Corby, B., Shemmings, D. and Wilkins, D. (2005) *Child Abuse: An Evidence Base for Confident Practice*, 4th edn, Maidenhead, Open University Press.

Crossley, M. (2006) *Contesting Psychiatry: Social Movements in Mental Health*, London, Routledge.

Dallos, R. (2006) *Attachment Narrative Therapy: Integrating Narrative, Systemic and Attachment Therapies*, Maidenhead, Open University Press.

Daniel, B. and Wassell, S. (2002) *The School Years: Assessing and Promoting Resilience in Vulnerable Children*, London, Jessica Kingsley.

Desai, S. (2018) 'Solution-focused Practice', in Thompson and Stepney (2018).

Day, R. C. and Hamblin, R. L. (1964) 'Some Effects of Close and Punitive styles of Supervision', *American Journal of Sociology*, 69, pp. 499-510.

Dingwall, R., Eekelaar, J. and Murray, T. (1983) *Protection of Children: State Intervention and Family Life*, Oxford, Blackwell.

Doka, K. (ed.) (1989) *Disenfranchised Grief*, Lexington, MA, Lexington Books.

Doka, K. (ed.) (2001) *Disenfranchised Grief: New Directions, Challenges, and Strategies for Practice*, Champaign, IL, Research Press.

Dorling, D. (2015) *Injustice: Why Social Inequality Still Persists*, 2nd edn., Bristol, The Policy Press.

Durkheim, E. (2006) *On Suicide*, London, Penguin (originally published 1897).

Dutton, D. G. (2007) *The Abusive Personality: Violence and Control in Intimate Relationships*, 2nd edn, New York, NY, Guilford Press.

Dutton, D. G. and Bodnarchuck, M. (2005) 'Through a Psychological Lens: Personality and Spouse Assault' in Loseke *et al*. (pp. 5-18).

Earley, L. and Cushway, D. (2002) 'The Parentified Child', *Clinical Child Psychology and Psychiatry*, (2).

Eiseley, L. (1969) *The Unexpected Universe,* New York, Harcourt, Brace and World.

Fahlberg, V. (1994) *A Child's Journey through Placement*, London, British Association for Adoption and Fostering.

Ferguson, H. (2004) *Protecting Children in Time*, Basingstoke, Palgrave Macmillan.

Ferguson, H. (2011) *Child Protection Practice*, Basingstoke, Palgrave Macmillan.

Fineman, S. (ed.) (2000) *Emotion in Organizations*, 2nd edn, London, Sage.

Fischer, A. (2000) *Gender and Emotion: Social Psychological Perspectives*, Cambridge, Cambridge University Press.

Flaskas, C. (2007) 'The Balance of Hope and Hopelessness', in Flaskas *et al*. (2007).

Flaskas, C., McCarthy, I. and Sheehan, J. (eds) (2007) *Hope and Despair in Narrative and Family Therapy, Adversity, Forgiveness and Reconciliation*, London, Routledge.

Gadamer, H. G. (2013) *Truth and Method*, London, Bloomsbury.

Gilbert, P. (2005) *Leadership: Being Effective and Remaining Human*, Lyme Regis, Russell House Publishing.

Gilbreath, B. (2004) 'Creating Healthy Workplaces: The Supervisor's Role', in Cooper and Robertson (2004).

Gillett, L. (2011) *Surviving Schizophrenia: A Memoir*, Christchurch, Twynham Press.

Hancock, P., Simmons, S. and Whitwell, J. (1990) 'The Importance of Food in Relation to the Treatment of Deprived and Disturbed Children in Care', *International Journal of Therapeutic Communities*, 11 (2), pp. 103-11.

Harms, L. (2018) 'Narrative Approaches', in Thompson and Stepney (2018).

Harvey, J. H. (2002) *Perspectives on Loss and Trauma: Assaults on the Self*, Thousand Oaks, Sage.

Hesketh, I. and Cooper, C. (2019) *Wellbeing at Work: How to Design, Implement and Evaluate an Effective Strategy*, London, Kogan Page.

Hochschild, A. (1983) *The Managed Heart: Commercialization of Human Feelings*, Berkeley, University of California Press.

Holloway, M. and Moss, B. (2010) *Spirituality and Social Work*, Basingstoke, Palgrave Macmillan.

Hooper, L. M. (2007) 'Expanding the Discussion Regarding Parentification and its Varied Outcomes: Implications for Mental Health Research and Practice', *Journal of mental Health Counseling*, 29(4).

Horwath, J. (ed.) (2010) *The Child's World: The Comprehensive Guide to Assessing Children in Need*, 2nd edn, London, Jessica Kingsley.

Hosin, A. A. (ed.) (2007) *Responses to Traumatized Children*, Basingstoke, Palgrave Macmillan.

Howe, D. (2005) *Child Abuse and Neglect: Attachment, Development and Intervention*, Basingstoke, Palgrave Macmillan.

Howe, D. (2011) *Attachment Across the Lifecourse: A Brief Introduction*, Basingstoke, Palgrave Macmillan.

Howe, D., Brandon, M., Hinings, D. and Schofield, G. (1999) *Attachment Theory, Child Maltreatment and Family Support*, Basingstoke, Macmillan.

James, B. (1994) *Handbook for Treatment of Attachment-Trauma Problems in Children*, New York, NY, The Free Press.

James, B. (2009) *Treating Traumatized Children*, New York, NY, The Free press.

Jackson, R., Jarvis, L., Gunning, J, and Breen-Smyth, M. (2011) *Terrorism: A Critical Introduction*, Basingstoke, Palgrave Macmillan.

Johnson, S. M. (2019) *Attachment Theory in Practice: Emotionally Focused Therapy (EFT) with Individuals, Couples, and Families*, New York, Guilford Press.

Johnston, J., Roseby, V. and Kuehnle, K. (2009) *In the Name of the Child: A Developmental Approach to Understanding and Helping Children of Conflicted and Violent Divorce*, New York, NY, Springer Publishing Company.

Kahn, W. A. (2005) *Holding Fast: The Struggle to Create Resilient Caregiving Organizations*, New York, Brunner-Routledge.

Kelloway, E. K., Teed, M. and Prosser, M. (2008) 'Leading to a Healthy Workplace', in Kinder *et al.* (2008).

Kinder, A., Hughes, R. and Cooper, C. L. (eds) (2008) *employee Well-being Support: A Workplace Resource*, Chichester, Wiley.

Levy, T. and Orlans, M. (1998) *Attachment, Trauma and Healing: Understanding and Treating Attachment Disorder in Children and Families*, Washington DC, Child Welfare League of America.

Loseke, D. R. Gelles, R. J. and Cavanaugh, M. M. (eds) (2005) *Current Controversies on Family Violence*, Thousand Oaks, CA, Sage.

May, V. M. (2015) *Pursuing Intersectionality: Unsettling Dominant Imaginaries*. New York, Routledge.

McDonald, C. (2009) 'Children and Poverty: Why their Experience of their Lives Matters for Policy', *Australian Journal of Social Issues*, 44(1).

Minuchin, Minuchin, S, Montalvo, B., Rosman, B. and Schumer, F. (1967) *Families of the Slums*, New York, Basic Books.

Moeller. S. D. (1999) *Compassion Fatigue: How the Media Sell Disease, Famine, War and Death*, New York, Routledge.

Moss, B. (2005) *Spirituality and Religion*, Lyme Regis, Russell House Publishing.

Moss, B. (2009) Spirituality in the Workplace. In: Thompson, N. and Bates, J. (eds) (2009) *Promoting Workplace Well-being,* Basingstoke, Palgrave. Macmillan.

Munro, E. (2008) *Effective Child Protection*, 2nd edn, London, Sage.

Munro, E. (2011) *The Munro Review of Child Protection: Final Report: A Child-centred System*, London, The Stationery Office.

Neimeyer, R. A. (ed.) (2001) *Meaning Reconstruction and the Experience of Loss*, Washington, American Psychological Society.

Neimeyer, R. A. and Levitt, H. (2001) 'Coping and Coherence: A Narrative Perspective on Resilience', in Snyder (2001).

Neimeyer, R. A. and Anderson, A. (2002) 'Meaning Reconstruction', in Thompson (2002).

Neimeyer, R. A. (2010)

Offermann, L. R. and Hellman, P. S. (1996) 'Leadership Behavior and Subordinate Stress: A 360° View', *Journal of Occupational Health Psychology*, 1, pp. 382-390.

Ogden, P., Minton, K. and Pain, C. (2006) *Trauma and the Body*, New York, W. W. Norton.

Ong, B. N. (1985) 'The Paradox of "Wonderful Children": The Case of Child Abuse', *Early Childhood Development and Care*, 21.

Papadatou, D. (2009) *In the Face of Death: Professionals who Care for the Dying and Bereaved*, New York, Springer.

Payne, M. (2006) *Narrative Therapy*, 2nd edn, London, Sage.

Percy-Smith, B. and Thomas, N. (eds) (2009) *A Handbook of Children and Young People's Participation: Perspectives from Theory and Practice*, London, Routledge.

Perry, B. D. and Szalavitz, M. (2017) *The Boy Who Was Raised as a Dog and Other Stories from a Child Psychiatrist's Notebook,* 3rd edn, New York, Basic Books.

Pozzulo, J. and Bennell, C. (2019) *Working with Trauma-Exposed Children and Adolescents: Evidence-Based and Age-Appropriate Practices*, London, Routledge.

Prior, V. and Glaser, D. (2006) *Understanding Attachment and Attachment Disorders: Theory, Evidence and Practice*, London, Jessica Kingsley Publishers.

Prout, A. (2002) 'Researching Children as Social Actors: An Introduction to the Children 5-16 Programme', *Children and Society*, 12, pp. 67-76.

Pughe, B. and Philpot, T. (2007) *Living Alongside a Child's Recovery: Therapeutic Parenting with Traumatized Children*, London, Jessica Kingsley.

Quitangon, G. (2015) *Vicarious Trauma and Disaster Mental Health: Understanding Risks and Promoting Resilience*, New York, Routledge.

Raphael, B. (1990) *When Disaster Strikes: A Handbook for the Caring Professions*, London, Unwin Hyman.

Richman, J. A., Flaherty, J. A., Rospenda, K. M. and Christensen, M. (1992) 'Medical Health Consequences and Correlates of Medical Student Abuse', *Journal of the American Medical Association*, 267, pp. 692-694.

Robertson, I. and Cooper, C. (2011) *Well-being: Productivity and Happiness at Work*, Basingstoke, Palgrave Macmillan.

Robertson, I. and Tinline, G. (2009) 'Understanding and Improving Psychological Well-being for Individual and Organizational Effectiveness', in Kinder *et al.* (2009).

Robinson, K. H. and Jones Diaz, C. (2006) *Diversity and Difference in Early Childhood*

Rogers, C. (1960) *On Becoming a Person: A Therapist's View of Psychotherapy*, London, Constable.

Rogers, A. and Pilgrim, D. (2014) *A Sociology of Mental Health and Illness*, 5th edn, Maidenhead, Open University Press.

Rose, R. (2012) *Life Story Therapy with Traumatized Children: A Model for Practice*, London, Jessica Kingsley Publishing.

Rose, R. (ed.) (2017) *Innovative Therapeutic Life Story Work: Developing Trauma-Informed Practice for Working with Children, Adolescents and Young Adults*, London, Jessica Kingsley Publishers.

Rose. R. and Philpot, T. (2005) *The Child's Own Story: Life Story Work with Traumatized Children*, London, Jessica Kingsley.

Rothschild, B. with Rand, M. (2006) *Help for the Helper: Self-care Strategies for Managing Burnout and Stress*, London and New York, W.W. Norton.

Rustin, M. and Quagliata, E. (eds) (2004) *Assessment in Child Psychotherapy*, London and New York, Karnac.

Rymaszewska, J. and Philpot, T. (2006) *Reaching the Vulnerable Child: Therapy with Traumatized Children*, London, Jessica Kingsley.

Saleebey, D. (2008) *The Strengths Perspective in Social Work Practice*, 5th edn., London, Pearson.

Sangster, K. L. and Lee, A. (2017) 'Spirituality and Traumatic Loss: Pathways to Healing through Spiritual Classics and Focusing', in Thompson and Cox (2017).

Schiraldi, G. R. (1999) *The Post-Traumatic Stress Disorder Sourcebook: A Guide to Healing, Recovery and Growth*, London, McGraw-Hill.

Schnall, P. L., Dobson, M and Rosskam, E. (eds) (2009) *Unhealthy Work: Causes, Consequences, Cures*, Amityville, NY, Baywood.

Schneider, J. M. (1994) *Finding My Way*, Colfax, WI, Seasons Press.

Schneider, J. M. (2000) *The Overdiagnosis of Depression: Recognizing Grief and its Transformational Potential*, Traverse City, MI, Seasons Press.

Schneider, J. M. (2012) *Finding My Way: From Trauma to Transformation: The Journey through Loss and Grief*, 2nd edn, Traverse City, MI, Seasons Press.

Schön, D. F. (1983) *The Reflective Practitioner*, New York, Basic Books.

Scott, M. J. (2008) *Moving On After Trauma: A Guide for Survivors, Family and Friends*, Hove, Routledge.

Seebohm, F. (1968) *Report of the Committee on Local Authority and Allied Personal Social Services*, London, HMSO.

Smith, M. and Fulcher, L. (2013) *Residential Child Care in Practice: Making a Difference*, Bristol, The Policy Press.

Snyder, R. (ed.) (2001) *Coping with Stress*, New York, Oxford University Press.

Solomon, M. and Siegel, D. J. (eds) (2003) *Healing Trauma: Attachment, Mind, Body and Brain*, New York, W.W. Norton.

Stewart, A. (1994) 'The Grief of the Abused Male', paper presented at the Helping the Bereaved Male conference, London, Ontario, Canada, May.

Stroebe, M. and Schut, H. (1999) 'The Dual Process Model of Coping with Bereavement: Rationale and Description', *Death Studies* **23** (3).

Stroebe, M., Schut, H. and van den Bout, J. (eds) (2012) *Complicated Grief: Scientific Foundations for Health Care Professionals*, London, Routledge.

Tait, A. and Wosu, H. (2013) *Direct Work with Vulnerable Children: Playful Activities and Strategies for Communication*, London, Jessica Kingsley Publishers.

Taleb, N. N. (2010) *The Black Swan: The Impact of the Highly Improbable*, New York, Random House.

Tedeschi, R., Park, C. and Calhoun, L. (eds) (1998) *Posttraumatic Growth: Positive Changes in the Aftermath of Crisis*, Mahweh, NJ, Lawrence Erlbaum.

Thomas, M. and Philpot, T. (2009) *Fostering a Child's Recovery: Family Placement for Traumatized Children*, London, Jessica Kingsley.

Thompson, N. (1999) 'Responding to loss', in Bates *et al.* (1999).

Thompson, N. (2000) *Theory and Practice in Human Services*, 2nd edn, Buckingham, Open University Press.

Thompson, N. (2002) *Building the Future: Social Work with Children, Young People and their Families*, Lyme Regis, Russell House Publishing.

Thompson, N. (2004) *Group Care with Children and Young People*, 2nd edn, Lyme Regis, Russell House Publishing.

Thompson, S. (2005) *Age Discrimination*, Lyme Regis, Russell House Publishing.

Thompson, N. (2007) *Power and Empowerment*, Lyme Regis, Russell House.

Thompson, N. (2008) 'Focusing on Outcomes: Developing Systematic Practice', *Practice: Social Work in Action*, 20(1).

Thompson, N. (2009) *Loss, Grief and Trauma in the Workplace*, New York, Routledge.

Thompson, N. (2011) *Crisis Intervention*, 2nd edn, Lyme Regis, Russell House Publishing.

Thompson, N. (2012) *Grief and its Challenges*, Basingstoke, Palgrave Macmillan.

Thompson, N. (2013) *People Management*, Basingstoke, Palgrave Macmillan.

Thompson, N. (2015) *Understanding Social Work: Preparing for Practice*, 4th edn, London, Palgrave.

Thompson, N. (2016a) *The Authentic Leader*. London, Palgrave.

Thompson, N. (2016b) *Anti-discriminatory Practice: Equality, Diversity and Social Justice*, 6th edn, London, Palgrave.

Thompson, N. (2017a) *Theorizing Practice*, 2nd edn, London, Palgrave.

Thompson, N. (2017b) *Social Problems and Social Justice*, London, Palgrave.

Thompson, N. (2017c) 'Traumatic Grief: An Existentialist Perspective', in Thompson and Cox (2017).

Thompson, S. (2017d) 'Old Age and Assaults on the Self: A Disenfranchised Form of Trauma?', in Thompson *et al.* (2017).

Thompson, N. (2018a) *Effective Communication: A Guide for the People Professions*, 3rd edn, London, Palgrave.

Thompson, N. (2018b) *Applied Sociology*, New York, Routledge.

Thompson, N. (2018c) *Promoting Equality: Working with Diversity and Difference*, 4th edn, London, Palgrave.

Thompson, N. (2019a) *Mental Health and Well-being: Alternatives to the Medical Model*, New York, Routledge.

Thompson, S. (2019b) *The Care of Older People Practice Manual*, Wrexham, Avenue Media Solutions.

Thompson, N. and Bates, J. (eds) (2009) *Promoting Workplace Well-being*, Basingstoke, Palgrave Macmillan.

Thompson, N., Cox, G. R. and Stevenson, R. (eds) (2017) *Handbook of Traumatic Loss: A Guide to Theory and Practice*, New York, Routledge.

Thompson, N. and Cox, G. R. (eds) (2020) *Promoting Resilience: Responding to Adversity, Vulnerability, Loss, and Grief*, New York, Routledge.

Thompson, N. and Gilbert, P. (2019) *Reflective Supervision: A Learning and Development Manual*, 2nd edn, Hove, Pavilion Publishing.

Thompson, N. and Stepney, P. (eds) (2018) *Social Work Theory and Methods: The Essentials*, New York, Routledge.

Thompson, N. and Walsh, M. (2010) 'The Existential Basis of Trauma', *Journal of Social Work Practice* 24(4).

Thompson, S. and Thompson, N. (2018) *The Critically Reflective Practitioner*, 2nd edn, London, Palgrave.

Thompson, S. and Wallace, R. (2012) *Tackling Low Self-esteem: Building Confidence and Self-respect*, e-book published by Avenue Media Solutions.

Tomlinson, P. (2004) *Therapeutic Approaches in Work with Traumatized Children and Young People: Theory and Practice*, London, Jessica Kingsley.

Tomlinson, P. and Philpot, T. (2008) *A Child's Journey to Recovery: Assessment and Planning with Traumatized Children*, London, Jessica Kingsley.

Townsend, J., Phillips, J. and Elkins, T. J. (2000) 'Employee Retaliation: The Neglected Consequence of Poor Leader-Member Exchange Relations', *Journal of Occupational Health Psychology*, 5, pp. 457-63.

Trowell, J. (2004) 'Assessing Sexually Abused Children', in Rustin and Quagliata (2004).

Ussher, J. (2011) *The Madness of Women*, Abingdon, Routledge.

Vaughan, J. (2003) 'The Rationale for the Intensive Programme', in Archer and Burnell (2003).

Van der Kolk, B. (2015) *The Body Keeps the Score: Mind, Brain and Body in the Transformation of Trauma*, London, Penguin.

Walsh, M. (2001) *The Kite that Couldn't Fly*, Montford Bridge, SACCS.

Walsh, M. (2009) 'Foreword', in Thomas and Philpot (2009).

Walsh, M. and Thompson, N. (2017) 'Responding to Childhood Trauma', in Thompson and Cox (2017).

Waterhouse, R. (2000) *Lost in Care: Report of the Tribunal of Inquiry into the Abuse of Children in Care in the Former County Council Areas of Gwynedd and Clwyd since 1974*, London, The Stationery Office.

Weld, N. (2009) *Making Sure Children Get 'Held'*, Lyme Regis, Russell House Publishing.

Winnicott, D. W. (1949) 'Birth Memories, Birth Trauma and Anxiety', in Winnicott (2002).

Winnicott, D. W. (2002) *Through Paediatrics to Psychanalysis*, London, Karnac Books.

Witcher, S. (2013) *Inclusive Equality: A Vision for Social Justice*, Bristol, The Policy Press.

Ziegler, D. (2002) *Traumatic Experience and the Brain: A handbook for Understanding and Treating those Traumatized as Children*, Phoenix, AZ, Acacia Publishing.

Appendices

Appendix I: Guide to further learning

Books

Mary was involved in the development of a set of five books, each of which covered an important aspects of trauma and recovery for abused children.

The SACCS series

Pughe, B. and Philpot, T. (2007) *Living Alongside a Child's Recovery: Therapeutic Parenting with Traumatized Children*, London, Jessica Kingsley.

Rose. R. and Philpot, T. (2005) *The Child's Own Story: Life Story Work with Traumatized Children*, London, Jessica Kingsley.

Rymaszewska, J. and Philpot, T. (2006) *Reaching the Vulnerable Child: Therapy with Traumatized Children*, London, Jessica Kingsley.

Thomas, M. and Philpot, T. (2009) *Fostering a Child's Recovery: Family Placement for Traumatized Children*, London, Jessica Kingsley.

Tomlinson, P. and Philpot, T. (2008) A Child's Journey to Recovery: Assessment and Planning with Traumatized Children, London, Jessica Kingsley.

In addition, Patrick Tomlinson, formerly of SACCS, is the author of:

Tomlinson, P. (2004) *Therapeutic Approaches in Work with Traumatized Children and Young People: Theory and Practice*, London, Jessica Kingsley.

and the co-author of:

Barton, S., Gonzalez, R. and Tomlinson, P. (2012) *Therapeutic Residential Care for Children and Young People: An Attachment and Trauma-Informed Model for Practice*, London, Jessica Kingsley.

Child protection

The child protection or 'safeguarding' field has an extensive literature base. Some of the key texts are:

Corby, B., Shemmings, D. and Wilkins, D. (2012) *Child Abuse: An Evidence Base for Confident Practice*, 4th edn, Maidenhead, Open University Press.

Ferguson, H. (2011) *Child Protection Practice*, Basingstoke, Palgrave Macmillan.

Munro, E. (2008) *Effective Child Protection*, London, Sage.

Trauma

This is also a field with a very large literature base. A key text is:

Thompson, N., Cox, G. R. and Stevenson, R. (eds) (2017) *Handbook of Traumatic Loss: A Guide to Theory and Practice*, New York, Routledge.

Other important texts include:

Bracken, P. (2002) *Trauma: Culture, Meaning and Philosophy*, London, Whurr.

Harvey, J. H. (2002) *Perspectives on Loss and Trauma: Assaults on the Self*, London, Sage.

Perry, B. D. and Szalavitz, M. (2017) *The Boy Who Was Raised as a Dog and Other Stories from a Child Psychiatrist's Notebook,* 3rd Edn, New York, Basic Books.

Thompson, N. (2009) *Loss, Grief and Trauma in the Workplace*, New York, Routledge.

Ziegler, D. (2002) *Traumatic Experience and the Brain: A Handbook for Understanding and Treating those Traumatized as Children*, Phoenix, AZ, Acacia Publishing.

Therapeutic approaches

There is a long history of published work devoted to therapeutic work with children. We present just a selection from the vast library of work available.

Bannister, A. (2003) *Creative Therapies with Traumatized Children*, London, Jessica Kingsley.

Barton, S. Gonzalez, R. and Tomlinson, P. (2012) *Therapeutic Residential Care for Children and Young People. An Attachment and Trauma-Informed Model for Practice*. London, Jessica Kingsley Publishers.

Bettelheim. B. (1970) *The Children of the Dream*, New York, Avon Books.

Bion, W. R. (1962) *Learning from Experience*, London, Karnac.

Bowlby, J. (1969) *Attachment and Loss: Vol 1 Attachment*, London, Hogarth Press.

Bowlby, J. (1979) *The Making and Breaking of Affectional Bonds*, London, Tavistock.

Bronfenbrenner, U. (1979) *The Ecology of Human Development: Experiments by Nature and Design*, Cambridge, MA, Harvard University Press.

Cairns, B. (2016) *Attachment Trauma and Resilience: Therapeutic Caring for Children*. London, BAAF.

Calhoun, L. G. and Tedeschi, R. G. (1999) *Facilitating Posttraumatic Growth*, Mahwah, NJ, Lawrence Erlbaum Associates.

Crossley, M. L. (2000) *Introducing Narrative Psychology: Self, Trauma and the Construction of Meaning*, Maidenhead, Open University Press.

Dallos, R. (2006) *Attachment Narrative Therapy: Integrating Narrative, Systemic and Attachment Therapies*, Maidenhead, Open University Press.

Daniel, B. and Wassell, S. (2002) *The School Years: Assessing and Promoting Resilience in Vulnerable Children*, London, Jessica Kingsley.

Dockar-Drysdale, B. (1990) *The Provision of Primary Experience: Winnicottian Work with Children and Adolescents*, London, Free Association Books.

Elliott, A., (2013) *Why Can't My Child Behave: Empathic Parenting Strategies that Work for Adoptive and Foster Families*. London, Jessica Kingsley Publishers.

Emond, R. and Steckley, L. (2016), *A Guide to Therapeutic Child Care: What you Need to Know about a Healing Home*. London, Jessica Kingsley Publishers.

Geldard, K., Geldard, D., Yin Foo, R. (2016) *Counselling Adolescents: The Proactive Approach for Young People*. Fourth Edition. London, SAGE Publications.

Gilligan, R. (2009) *Promoting Resilience: Supporting Children and Young People who are in Care, Adopted or in Need*. London, British Association for Adoption and Fostering.

Nicholson, C. Irwin, Michael, Dwivedi, K, N. (2010) *Children and Adolescents in Trauma. Creative Therapeutic Approaches*. London, Jessica Kingsley.

North, J. (2013) *Mindful Therapeutic Care for Children: A Guide to Reflective Practice*, London, Jessica Kingsley.

Rose, R. (2017) *Innovative Therapeutic Life Story Work: Developing Trauma-Informed Practice for Working with Children, Adolescents and Young Adults*, London, Jessica Kingsley Publishers.

Steele, W. Malchiodi, C. (2012), *Trauma-Informed Practices with Children and Adolescents*. East Sussex, Routledge.

Taylor, C. (2012) *Empathic Care for Children with Disorganized Attachments: A Model for Mentalizing, Attachment and Trauma-Informed Care*. London, Jessica Kingsley.

Treisman, K. (2017) *Working with Relational and Developmental Trauma in Children and Adolescents*. London, Routledge.

Attachment

Attachment theory is a key underpinning of the theory base informing trauma recovery.

Howe, D. (2005) *Child Abuse and Neglect: Attachment, Development and Intervention*, Basingstoke, Palgrave Macmillan.

Howe, D. (2011) *Attachment Across the Lifecourse: A Brief Guide*, Basingstoke, Palgrave Macmillan.

Prior, V. and Glaser, D. (2006) *Understanding Attachment and Attachment Disorders: Theory, Evidence and Practice*, London, Jessica Kingsley Publishers.

Taylor, C. (2010) *Caring for Children and Teenagers with Attachment Difficulties*. London, Jessica Kingsley.

Equality, diversity and inclusion

This is yet another field that now has a large literature base, although it was not always so, as the complex and sensitive issues involved were neglected for many years. Neil has published extensively in this area:

Thompson, N. (2016) *Anti-discriminatory Practice: Equality, Diversity and Social Justice*, 6th edn, London, Palgrave.

Thompson, N. (2017) *Social Problems and Social Justice*, London, Palgrave.

Thompson, N. (2018) *Promoting Equality: Working with Diversity and Difference*, 4th edn, London, Palgrave.

Thompson, N. (2019) *Promoting Equality, Valuing Diversity: A Learning and Development Manual*, 2nd edn, Hove, Pavilion Publishing.

Other important works include:

Bhatti-Sinclair, K. and Smethurst, C. (eds) (2017) *Diversity, Difference and Dilemmas: Analysing Concepts and Developing Skills*, London, Open University Press.

James, A. and Prout, A. (eds). (2015) *Constructing and Reconstructing Childhood: Contemporary Issues in the Sociological Study of Childhood*. London, Routledge

Mullaly, B. and Dupré, M. (2019) *The New Structural Social Work*, 4th edn, Toronto, Oxford University Press.

Robinson, K. H. and Jones Diaz, C. (2006) *Diversity and Difference in Early Childhood Education: Issues for Theory and Practice*, Maidenhead, Open University Press.

Workplace well-being (caring for the carers)

A once neglected field, it is now starting to get the attention it deserves.

Renzenbrink, I. (ed.) (2011) *Caregiver Stress and Staff Support in Illness, Dying and Bereavement*, Oxford, Oxford University Press.

Rothschild, B. with Rand, M. (2006) *Help for the Helper: Self-care Strategies for Managing Burnout and Stress*, London and New York, W.W. Norton.

Thompson, N. (2013) *People Management*, Basingstoke, Palgrave Macmillan.

Thompson, N. and Bates, J. (2009) *Promoting Workplace Well-being*, Basingstoke, Palgrave Macmillan.

Training and Online Learning Resources

Mary and Neil have developed a set of e-learning courses that are very relevant to what is discussed in this book:

Childhood Trauma and Recovery
Communicating with Children
Safeguarding Children from Abuse
Sexual Abuse and Childhood Sexuality

These are available from: www.avenuemediasolutions.com/shop.

Websites and organisations

Barnardo's https://www.barnardos.org.uk/

BASPCAN for Child Protection Professionals https://www.baspcan.org.uk/membership/

Institute of Recovery from Childhood Trauma https://irct.org.uk/

International Society for Traumatic Stress Studies

http://www.istss.org/public-resources/what-is-childhood-trauma.aspx

The National Child Traumatic Stress Network

https://www.nctsn.org/what-is-child-trauma/trauma-types/early-childhood-trauma

NSPCC https://www.nspcc.org.uk/

Appendix II: The children's stories

Here we present a small number of brief accounts of important elements of the stories of some of the children Mary and her team have worked with and helped on the road to recovery. Our intention is to provide these and the questions that follow each one as exercises that can be used either by individuals as part of their personal study or by groups on training courses or as part of a college or university programme of study. We hope they will provide you with plenty of food for thought and that you will find them useful.

As you consider the questions that follow each cameo, please think very carefully about them. The object of the exercise is to encourage you to think deeply about the key issues involved. So it is your considered response that is needed, not just your initial reaction.

Charlie's story

Charlie came to live at one of Mary's houses when he was six years old. By that time he had been removed from home because he had been sexually, physically and emotionally abused by his father and probably his mother as well. He had subsequently had 53 placements in various foster homes.

The poor child did not know what a mother was, let alone which one was which.

His inner world was chaotic, and it took a long time before he could trust that he was going to be with us tomorrow.

Sadly, Charlie's story is extreme, but by no means uncommon. Serial placements should be seen as the atrocities that they are, and children who have already been traumatised by what has happened to them at home should not have to live through this further assault on their lives.

What we can learn from Charlie's story…

1. What circumstances could have led to Charlie having so many placement breakdowns?

2. What could potentially have been done to prevent so many changes in home circumstances for Charlie?

3. What impact is 53 changes of placement likely to have on such a young child?

4. Could allowing so many changes to happen be considered a form of abuse? If so, why?

5. Are there any other lessons we can learn from Charlie's experiences?

Jenny's story

Jenny was the youngest of four children. She had two older brothers and an older sister. She was three-years old when I met her. The other children told me through play that they all slept in the marital bed where there were no sexual boundaries with their parents or with each other. Their parents sexually abused them and encouraged them to be sexual with each other.

Jenny was highly eroticised in her foster family, and when it became apparent that sex was not going to happen to her there, she rubbed her tummy and genitals almost raw, such was her need to get some kind of sexual release. I feel sure that Jenny experienced sex as an integral part of parenting, and the withdrawal or absence of sex was intolerable for her.

Her foster mother also found it very difficult to accept that this three-year old was so eroticised, and it meant that she saw her very differently. This challenged the foster mother regarding her own sexuality and sexual feelings. Ultimately, the placement broke down because of these strong dynamics.

What we can learn from Jenny's story…

1. In what ways might a lack of sexual boundaries be considered harmful or problematic?
2. How might the experience have affected Jenny's 'internal model' and worldview?
3. Why might foster carers struggle to cope with an eroticised child like Jenny? What are the challenges involved?
4. What support or training might foster carers need in such circumstances?
5. Are there any other lessons we can learn from Jenny's experiences?

Sally's story

When Sally came to us she had had several different foster placements. She had lost touch with her siblings. Her parents had separated, and she no longer had any contact with them either. Somewhere along the way she had been given a different name. When she came to us she was withdrawn and did not really know who she was or what had happened to her.

I felt that she could not possibly move on until we had picked up the broken shards of her life and reconstructed them in a coherent way, so that she was able to understand who she was, and what had happened when and where. Only once she was able to assimilate this information and put it into some kind of perspective was she able to start looking forward again.

This is painstaking work, involving going through social services and other records, finding and interviewing immediate and extended family, past carers, teachers and anyone else who might have been significant. It means collecting stories, not just about the bad things that have happened, but all the little stories, some funny, some ordinary, some poignant. Stories about things that have happened to us when we are small that tell us a little bit about who we are, so important when we are trying to build our identity.

This work was to become the blueprint for our life story work. Every child who came to us had this experience, and when they left they each had a specially tailor-made book that they took with them into their next placement. In a retrospective study we did on children who had left us some time before, they all commented on how important that book was, and how they still treasure it.

What we can learn from Sally's story...

1. What impact is losing contact with her siblings and parents likely to have had on Sally?

2. Why is identity so important for children?

3. What do you see as the main benefits of life story work?

4. What problems might you have anticipated if Sally had not had the benefit of life story work?

5. Are there any other lessons we can learn from Sally's experiences?

Kerry's story

Kerry was two-years old when she was removed from her family. She had been subjected to all kinds of sexual behaviour at the hands of her father and maybe other uncles in the family. As far as we were aware, this had happened on a very regular basis. Kerry was placed in a foster family. Unfortunately for her, in her mind families were the most dangerous places and she acted as though she was still being abused. Her placement quickly broke down and she was taken to another family where the same thing happened.

Eventually, aged seven, she came to us, where she was able to live and be looked after in a house that was different from a family. There was not the same intensity of relationships, and the culture of all the houses was one of openness about sex not happening there. It took a long time before Kerry was able to trust and engage in the therapeutic process, but she was able to breathe and find some peace and her own space where she felt safe and contained. This meant that she was then able to build relationships with the new adults in her life, and her recovery started.

What we can learn from Kerry's story...

1. Why is it generally assumed that a family is the best place for children to grow up? In what circumstances might a family setting be less than ideal?

2. Why might children like Kerry continue to behave as though they were being abused after the abuse has stopped?

3. What could a residential placement offer that a family setting cannot?

4. What support and training would residential staff need to be able to parent an abused child effectively?

5. Are there any other lessons we can learn from Kerry's experiences?

Carl's story

Carl was six when he came to us. He looked like a displaced child. He was very small, had no teeth and his hair had fallen out. He had been sexually, physically and emotionally abused and neglected all his life.

When he arrived he was very sexualised, wanting to have sex with everything in the house; the curtains, the chairs, books, furniture. Gradually he settled down and that behaviour subsided, but in all that time he could look at a pebble, or a dandelion or a puddle and see a whole wonderful world. His sense of awe and wonder saved his life, I am sure.

What we can learn from Carl's story...

1. What effect is more than five years of abuse likely to have on a child's internal model or worldview?

2. How might that internal model shape their behaviour: (i) while still a child; and (ii) in their adult life if no recovery work were to be done?

3. How might each of the three elements of the Mary Walsh Approach (individual therapy; life story work; therapeutic parenting) contribute to changing that internal model in a positive direction?

4. In what ways might a (spiritual) sense of awe and wonder help a child cope with the aftermath of abuse?

5. Are there any other lessons we can learn from Carl's experiences?

Tracey's story

Tracey was a pretty, slim 12 year old. She came to us after a long history of abuse and being moved about in the care system. She was aggressive to others and to herself. Tracey felt she was responsible for the abuse and for all the consequences of that – for example, for her father going to prison, for the break up of her family and for the subsequent foster placement breakdowns.

She saw herself as intrinsically bad and she was full of shame and guilt.

She believed that she was fat and ugly, and no amount of reassurance could change these deep-seated beliefs.

What we can learn from Tracey's story...

1. Why might a child who has been traumatised by abuse become aggressive towards others?

2. Why might a child who has been traumatised by abuse become aggressive towards him- or herself?

3. What might lead a child to feel guilty if they have done nothing wrong?

4. Why would reassurance not change her deep-seated negative beliefs about herself?

5. Are there any other lessons we can learn from Tracey's experiences?

Becky's story

Becky was seven years old when we got to know her. She was the oldest child in her family and had been abused by her father for some time. Her mother had abdicated her role and Becky was seen in the family as her father's partner, and carer for the younger children.

When she came to us she did not know how to play. She wanted to dust and clean and spend time with the grown ups. She behaved as though she was 30. It took a long time to help her to see that it was good to be seven years old and enjoy being a child.

What we can learn from Becky's story...

1. What could motivate a father to sexually abuse his own daughter?
2. What pressures (such as domestic violence) might lead a mother to 'abdicate' her responsibility for a child?
3. What harm would it do a child to, in effect, be denied her childhood?
4. In what ways would being exposed to adult sexuality affect a child of seven?
5. Are there any other lessons we can learn from Becky's experiences?

Appendix III: The Mary Walsh Approach in a nutshell

- Children, especially young children, are vulnerable and in need of protection, too immature to do without adult support and nurturance.

- Tragically, many children find themselves in circumstances where they do not receive such protection and are subject to abuse of one form or another. To add insult to injury, it will often be one or both parents (who should be providing the protection) who are actually inflicting the abuse.

- Young children who do not understand what is happening to them will face immense confusion, turmoil, fear – even to the point of terror – anxiety, physical symptoms (stomach disorders, for example) and other signs of extreme stress.

- The net result of this is likely to be trauma, a psychological injury that can be just as harmful as a physical injury, if not more so. To be more precise, it is a psychosocial and existential injury – social because it has both social roots and social consequences, and existential because it affects our very sense of who we are and how we fit into the world.

- The existential nature of childhood trauma can leave a child uncertain of who they are and what is expected of them. In particular, it can leave them feeling totally unsafe, vulnerable to the point of extreme distress.

- Traditionally, it has been thought that, provided the abused child was removed from the harmful situation and placed in a loving, caring, nurturing substitute home, they would eventually 'get over' their trauma and have the opportunity to resume a 'normal' childhood.

- The work of Mary Walsh and her colleagues is built on the rejection of that assumption. It is premised on the recognition that children who have been traumatised by abuse will need to go through a process of recovery if they are to achieve some degree of quality of life and freedom from the adverse effects of trauma.

■ To facilitate that process of recovery, a three-dimensional approach was developed, incorporating individual therapy, life story work and therapeutic parenting. This approach has proved to be very successful with a large number of children.

■ Practitioners involved in working with traumatised children therefore need appropriate training to ensure that they have a sound knowledge base of the complex issues involved. A general understanding of child care practice will not be enough.

■ Such practitioners will also need to have appropriate support to help them cope with the often intense demands of working in a context of the aftermath of abuse and trauma.

■ All of this practice needs to be undertaken in a spirit of being child centred. This is not simply the legal requirement that the child's needs must be paramount; it is a broader recognition that progress will not be made unless children are listened to, their needs recognised and addressed and their voices heard. This is the case for all children, but it is particularly important for children whose voices were at one time silenced by abuse.